Dear Sarah

WILLIAM LORD HOUSE, KENNEBUNK

Dear Sarah

New England ice to the Orient and other incidents from the Journals of Captain Charles Edward Barry to his wife

by
Norman E. Borden Jr.

 THE BOND WHEELWRIGHT COMPANY, FREEPORT, MAINE

To *E. C. B.*

The First Congregational Church of Kennebunk (Unitarian) as it appeared in Captain Barry's day. This photograph was made sometime prior to 1900. The church is on Main Street, approximately across the street from William Lord's brick store.

Photo courtesy of The Brick Store Museum

PREFACE

IN A WAY, this book is a family affair. But it is an affair that I feel should be shared with all those who care for tales of the sea and adventurous living as it was practiced approximately a century and a quarter ago.

Until rather recently, I had always taken my great-grandfather, Charles Edward Barry, pretty much for granted. To be sure, I knew that he had been a sea captain who sailed some of the old square-rigged ships that were an important and colorful part of America's heritage. And I was vaguely aware that the period in which he lived had probably been rather exciting. From time to time over the years, I had thumbed with mild curiosity through two large bound volumes that contained typewritten copies of letters that my seafaring ancestor had written to my great-grandmother during the many long months he was at sea. But my knowledge and interest concerning this fascinating gentleman never progressed beyond a half-hearted resolution to someday find out more about him.

Then, one day, I could stand the suspense no longer. With rugged determination, I threw the procrastination of twenty years out the window and commenced in earnest to try to learn what my great-grandfather Barry's story was all about. The ultimate result is this book. Once my research started, it did not take long to discover that life both at sea and ashore during the golden age of the American wooden sailing ship in the 1830-50 period was both thrilling and enchanting. Even in those days, times were changing rapidly and each new year of Captain Barry's life brought some new way of doing things. He was a man of intelligence, integrity, and character, who was deeply in love with his wife. In his writing, he expressed himself exceedingly well. Therefore, in putting together the account of his life and times, I have let him tell his own story as much as possible.

Captain Barry's letters were in the form of a continuing journal in which he wrote every few days about anything that suited his fancy. Upon reaching port at the end of a voyage, he would mail his journals home to Sarah, his wife. She, in turn, carefully preserved them, then passed them on to her heirs. In the early 1930's, Miss Edith C. Barry, to whom this book is dedicated and who is Captain Barry's granddaughter as well as my own esteemed and respected aunt, had the interest and foresight to have the letters, or journals, copied on a typewriter for easy reading and bound in the volumes I have mentioned.

In recounting the story of Captain Barry's life, I have endeavored to reconstruct the environment in which he lived with all possible accuracy. In this, my greatest asset has been the manner in which the captain wrote his journals. To help pass the time during the long weeks and months he was at sea, he often wrote at great length. In much of this writing, he reminisced in considerable detail about the events of the years gone by. Because of this, it has been possible to piece together most of the details of Captain Barry's early life and the events that lead up to his marriage and the voyages to India that followed. When the material in the letters was carefully sifted and sorted, a clear picture of Captain Barry himself, the things that happened to him, and the places he visited emerged.

But the captain's letters, alone, were not capable of providing all the background necessary to be able to describe early nineteenth century living both on land and at sea. For this, I had the freely given assistance of many knowing people. I am particularly grateful to the following persons whose patient and generous help has proved an indispensable asset: Curator Mrs. Donald Kimball of The Brick Store Museum, Kennebunk, Maine; Librarian Mrs. Jared Wood of the Mystic Seaport Museum, Mystic, Connecticut; marine historian and authority on Maine sailing ships Robert B. Applebee, Stockton Springs,

Maine; Director Ernest S. Dodge, Assistant Director M. V. Brewington, and marine historian Philip C. F. Smith of the Peabody Museum, Salem, Massachusetts; Professor of Economics and authority on early New England railroads James R. Nelson of Amherst College, Amherst, Massachusetts; and Mr. John Lomas of Holcombe (Lancashire), England, who kindly did the research and investigation necessary to confirm the location of the wreck of the ship *Oakland* as well as provide the information that enabled me to describe the hamlet in Wales where Captain Barry stayed.

A word should also be said in regard to some of the illustrations used in this book. Although daguerreotypes were commencing to become popular in the 1840-50 period during which Captain Barry made his most important voyages, photography as we know it today was just being invented. Contemporary photographs of the places and people mentioned in the book are therefore nonexistent. Instead, a number of drawings have been used to illustrate the text. With the exception of the sketches of men harvesting winter ice, these are the work of William Edward Barry, the eldest son of Captain and Sarah Barry.

As shown in the Epilogue, William Barry became a historian and architect. He was also a competent artist who carried small sketchbooks with him on many occasions. In these he made drawings of whatever took his eye. Many of the now priceless little books repose in The Brick Store Museum at Kennebunk. Those sketches by William Barry that proved applicable for use as illustrations were graciously made available by the museum for photocopying and reproduction herein.

The four ice-cutting scenes in Chapter II are drawings by an unknown artist. They appeared as illustrations for an article by Frederick Tudor on the subject of ice in an 1875 issue of *Scribner's Monthly* magazine. According to Tudor, the locale was Fresh Pond at Cambridge, Massachusetts.

Wapping, Connecticut
September 1, 1965

/s/ NORMAN E. BORDEN, JR.

- xi -

TABLE OF CONTENTS

LIST OF FULL-PAGE ILLUSTRATIONS

Editor's Note:

> *In making the selection of drawings by William Barry
> that are scattered throughout the margins of this book
> and occasionally serve as actual illustration of the text,
> we have tried to avoid anachronisms. On the whole, the
> scenes, houses, ships, places, and artifacts he sketched
> were little changed from those his father might have
> seen earlier.*

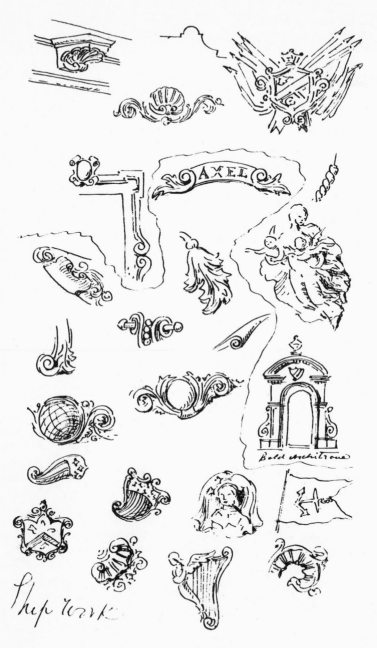

A page from one of William Barry's notebooks

PROLOGUE

Shipwreck

A strong southwest wind churned the water in St. George's Channel between the coast of Wales and Ireland's eastern shore on the morning of March 21, 1845. At mid-channel, due west of Saint David's Head and about one hundred miles southwest of Anglesey Island at the northwestern tip of Wales, a three-masted wooden sailing ship, bound for Liverpool, pitched and tossed in a moderately heavy sea. The seaman at her helm was holding a steady northeast by north course, which kept the wind almost directly astern. From time to time the sun broke through the low dark clouds that were chasing one another in rapid succession as they overtook and passed the vessel. Through occasional holes in the clouds, bright rays of sunlight glittered white on the ship's billowing square-rigged sails. A close look at the scroll on the transom of the vessel's square stern would have shown that this was the *Oakland,* out of Boston. Thirty-three days earlier the ship had left Charleston, South Carolina, her holds laden with bales of cotton for the spinning mills that fed the hungry looms of Lancashire.

Aboard the *Oakland,* sitting erect in a chair at a small desk in his finely paneled cabin, the ship's master was writing a letter. He was Charles Edward Barry, who, like the ship he commanded, also claimed Boston as his home port. While the morning wore on, he labored, completely absorbed in his writing in spite of

the handicap imposed by the rolling and bucking of the ship as she worked her way through the waves that the wind was driving up the channel.

Captain Barry was a small man who looked much older than the thirty-four years of age he actually was. He only weighed one hundred and twenty-five pounds, and when standing, he was but five feet, four inches tall. Nevertheless, and like many other small men, his natural aggressiveness more than made up for what he lacked in stature. His receding dark-brown hair exposed a high forehead. He was clean-shaven except for the long heavy sideburns that swept all the way down to his chin on each side of his wind-burned face. A long straight nose, blue-black penetrating eyes and a determined oval chin gave him the look of a man who inspired the respect of those who worked under him. And indeed he did. Although the crew of the *Oakland* knew Captain Barry as a tolerant and understanding master when occasion demanded, they also knew him as one who expected unquestioned obedience from everyone on board. His word was law and he enforced the law.

But Captain Barry was fair and he was just, for he thoroughly knew his business. His weathered complexion spoke more plainly than words of the many years he had spent at sea, learning his trade. At home and abroad, he was known for his ability to make a square-rigged sailing ship respond like a living thing to his handling. Under his supervision ships had a way of superbly doing whatever he asked of them. He was also known as an excellent navigator. Thomas Curtis, a prominent Boston merchant who was the *Oakland*'s principal owner, once stated that Captain Barry was " the best shipmaster to ever sail out of Boston."

A particularly violent lurch of the ship caused Captain Barry to look up from his writing. He glanced at the large pocket watch with a heavy gold case that was swinging with the motion of the ship on a hook in the wall above the desk. Noting that the time was approaching noon, he wiped the point of his pen with a small piece of chamois and placed the pen in its holder. Then, rising from his chair, he put away his papers. Captain

Barry had always disliked having to write at sea when the weather was rough. But he expected to reach Liverpool shortly after daylight the following morning and all mail had to be ready for posting by the time the anchor was dropped. After that, there would be no opportunity for writing. He put on his greatcoat, took his captain's cap from a peg on the wall, opened the cabin door, and went on deck.

At the charthouse Captain Barry removed a sextant from its storage box. A look at the ship's chronometer told him that it would be high noon in just three more minutes. It was the usual practice in those days to take a time sight at noon, when it was hoped that the ship's latitude might be established by catching a quick altitude of the sun just as it came to its zenith. But the accuracy of the method depended wholly upon the accuracy of the chronometer, which at best was subject to a small amount of error.

The captain carried the sextant to the forecastle (pronounced fo'c'sle) head where he took a stand beside the ship's lookout, who was stationed there. While he waited for the sun to come from behind a cloud, an apprentice boy — the youngest on the ship — commenced striking the bell on the poop deck, beside the helmsman. Eight strokes of the bell told all hands that the end of the forenoon watch had arrived. The call of eight bells was repeated by the lookout on the forecastle head, who struck a similar bell that hung within his easy reach. Men around the ship could be seen coming and going as the port watch relieved the starboard watch at their stations. The voice of the first mate, Thomas Curtis, Jr., who was the son of the *Oakland*'s principal owner, was heard as he gave his orders to the men of the port watch, of which he was in charge. There were seven seamen in his crew. The second mate and the members of his starboard watch quickly left the deck. The sun had come out briefly, and the captain had taken his sight. Soon all was quiet again, the only sound being the whistling of the wind in the rigging.

Back in the charthouse, Captain Barry carefully wiped droplets of salt water spray from the sextant before returning the

instrument to the box from which it had been removed. Then he took a copy of the 1841 edition of a book called *Practical Navigation*, by Nathaniel Bowditch, from its place in a rack. Leaning over the chart table, he consulted tables in the book and commenced making calculations on a sheet of paper. Like many of his contemporary Yankee shipmasters who were then setting the ship-handling standards of the world, Captain Barry could work " lunars " as well as Bowditch himself. Having established the ship's latitude, he computed the longitude. It was a tricky business, for any error made in the sun observation would bring a thirty-fold error in the result. But Captain Barry was a well-educated, careful, and experienced navigator who seldom made a mistake.

The door to the charthouse opened, and Curtis stepped inside. " How is our position, sir?" he asked.

"Very good, Mr. Curtis," replied the captain, looking up from a chart. " I make it out as latitude fifty-two degrees, four minutes north, by longitude five degrees, forty-five minutes west. You may instruct the helmsman to alter his course to northeast by three-quarters north. That should put us up on the Holyhead Light by midnight. There are strong northeast tidal currents near Anglesey, but I'm certain that I have allowed enough for them." [It should be noted that the Holyhead Light of the mid-nineteenth-century period is known as South Stack Light today. It marks some rocks on the most westerly extremity of Holy Island on the west coast of Anglesey.]

"Aye, I shall tell him," said Curtis, leaving the charthouse. By tradition, Captain Barry never gave orders directly to his men. All of his instructions were transmitted through the mate, who received them in private. It was the first mate who apportioned the work between the two watches, and it was he who saw to it that the captain's instructions were carried out to the letter. Except when getting underway at the start of a voyage, when tacking, reefing in a heavy blow, coming to anchor, or other ship's work that required "all hands," the captain did not appear in person to superintend the day's work at any time when the ship was at sea. In strict compliance with time-honored custom, the captain was never intimate with any of the crew, his first mate whom he had known since the man was a child being no exception. Curtis was the son of a man who had married a cousin of Captain Barry and was one of Captain Barry's very best friends.

The charthouse door opened again while the captain was still poring over his charts. Curtis had returned to enter the noon position in the ship's log, it being one of the mate's responsibilities to maintain the written account of all the details that formed the official record of the voyage. " I don't like the look of the weather, sir," he said. " The barometer's falling and the wind has increased."

" It will bear careful watching. I don't like it either. Be prepared to trim sail if it gets any worse," the captain replied. He went back to the deck, where he remained for quite a long while, glancing aloft from time to time, his professional eye noting with satisfaction the way the sails were drawing. The rigging was taut, the canvas in good condition, and the hull tight.

That the ship seemed to be rolling more violently than before did not worry Captain Barry. Though a bit unwieldy at times, the *Oakland* was a good ship and as stout as a man-of-war. And she was comparatively new, having been launched less than four years earlier, on May 13, 1841. The vessel had been built at Kennebunk, a maritime community on the coast of Maine, about twenty-five miles south of Portland. Besides the senior Thomas Curtis, two men named Thaddeus Nichols and Israel Whitney, both of Boston, also had an interest in the *Oakland*. Captain Barry had always been her master. A ship of 549 tons, her length overall was 145 feet; she had a 28-foot, 6-inch beam, and her draft when fully loaded, as she was now, was just a little over 13 feet. Her bluff burly bow and round kettle-shaped bottom were typical of the cotton-carrying ships of the period. Her clean, youthful-looking hull was painted dead-black, relieved only by a white waist that was checkered by black loading ports.

Captain Barry went on deck every half hour for the rest of the day to check on the ship and the weather. At dusk, he ordered the sails shortened, and at nine that evening, the mate came to his cabin to see him.

"The wind has increased to a full gale, sir, and we're shipping water over the deck," Curtis told the captain. He was standing just inside the cabin door, which he had closed behind him. Water dripped from his oilskins. His wet face was illuminated only by the reflected light of two candles that were burning in candle lamps fastened to the walls of the cabin. By the dim light of the candle nearest to his desk, Captain Barry had been re-reading what was obviously a small stack of old letters when the mate had knocked.

Several moments passed before Captain Barry answered. With more room, he would have ordered the ship hove-to under these conditions, but the water in St. George's Channel was too restricted for this. When he finally spoke, the captain said:  "Take in the sails on all masts. Leave only the headsails up to keep the ship with the wind. Even with the onshore current, the wind direction should carry the ship by Holyhead Light and Anglesey Island into the open water of the Irish Sea. I'll be on deck as soon as I get into my gear."

Below decks on their bunks in the forecastle, the men who had stood the second dog watch and had been relieved at 8:00 P.M. lay with their knees braced up to prop themselves against the rolling of the ship. They were trying to get what sleep they could before they went on duty again at midnight. It seemed to them that they had been below hardly any time at all when they were aroused by the first mate putting his head in the door and shouting: "All hands on deck to shorten sail!" The watch struggled sleepily into their oilskins in the crowded, muggy gloom of the forecastle. Minutes later, they were at their stations. Captain Barry was already on the poop, standing behind the helmsman.

The sky was now completely overcast. Except for the dull glow of the ship's whale-oil side lights and the lamp in the binnacle, the ship was as dark as a cave. The wind was blowing so hard that no one could walk along the pitching deck without steadying himself by holding on to something. Heavy seas were crashing aboard and a lifeline had been rigged from the forecastle head to the break of the poop. Occasionally, after a particularly heavy roll, only the poop and the forecastle head remained, like islands, above the swirl of foaming water. Fortunately, it was not a cold night for the time of year at this latitude.

The mate sent men from both watches aloft. Only three were assigned to each mast, as never more men than were strictly necessary were sent up into the rigging at any one time. The men started their climb aloft, scrambling up the wooden battens attached to the shrouds on the weather side of the ship so the wind would blow them on the rigging, not away from it into the sea. They went up swiftly. It was a long climb up the battens on the lower rigging, over the top of the spiders, then up again on the ratlines of the topmast rigging. They climbed over the crosstrees at the top of the masthead where the topgallant mast was stepped. Once the yard of the particular sail with which they were going to deal was reached, each group of three men on each of the masts swung on to the footrope, which was a rope running below each yard at just the right place for the men to stand.

With but little concern for the fact that their mast was jumping about and swinging far out over the boiling water of St. George's Channel more than one hundred feet below, the trio on a footrope — one at the center and one at each end of the yard — would pick up the sail that had been dropped by men who manned the braces on the deck below. They stowed the hard wet canvas (the spray from the waves crashing against the ship was driving that high), beating it with their fists to make it roll tight. As each sail was muzzled, the rolled canvas was made fast to the yard with canvas securing strips, called gaskets. It was difficult, dangerous work, but the men were used to it. With nothing but their own strength to keep them from falling, it was a severe test of skill and nerve. As was true of so many

jobs about a square-rigged sailing ship, it was a challenge to which perfection could be the only answer.

In a remarkably short time, considering the trying conditions under which the men had to work, all of the ship's canvas except the headsails had been stowed, and the off-duty watch went back to their bunks. The ship still continued to pitch and roll, but not as violently as before, and water no longer came over the deck. Even so, it was a bad night that might get worse. Captain Barry ordered the lookout doubled to pick up Holyhead Light the moment it came into view, and he did everything else that a captain could do to protect his ship. Then he returned to his cabin.

Two hours after midnight, the morning of March 22, the mate again rapped on Captain Barry's cabin door. When asked what was wanted, he said, " There's spindrift off the starboard bow, sir. We're getting close to land and Holyhead Light's not been sighted."

In almost no time the captain was on the poop. He took in the situation at a glance and ordered the helm to be put down immediately. He told the mate to send men to the fore-castle head to get ready to drop the anchor as soon as the ship came around into the wind and stopped her forward headway. But the *Oakland* had hardly commenced to come about when a shudder was felt throughout the ship. The shock quickly brought all hands on deck. The vessel took a list to starboard from which she did not recover. All forward motion ceased. " We're aground, sir," said Curtis, who had come to the poop to stand beside the captain. " What do you make of it?"

" We've hit a submerged rock off the northern coast of Wales, but I don't know where," Captain Barry replied. As he spoke, a giant wave came at the ship, keeling her over when it struck. The force of the mighty wall of water listed the ship dangerously. The deck stood at an angle of forty degrees, which submerged the starboard rail. Some of the cargo shifted. The time was 2:15 A.M., and the captain and every member of the crew knew that all hope for the ship had gone.

Captain Barry directed that the ship's boats be lowered,

but the starboard boats were already under water. The ship's longboat and the jolly boat, which were carried on the port side, were so high that they could not be easily launched. Happily, the *Oakland* showed no sign of sinking, listing further, or breaking up, so there was no apparent need for frantic haste. With great effort, skillful seamanship, and much good luck, both of the usable port boats were put over the side without getting smashed against the vessel's hull. It was decided to lower the longboat first. When it was a little more than halfway down, the line attached to the stern of the boat parted and the rear of the boat fell toward the water. The second mate and a seaman who had been riding the boat down were pitched headfirst into the sea. The current swept both men away into the night before anyone on board the ship could throw them a line.

Curtis, the first mate, who had been one of those holding the line aboard ship, lost his balance when the line broke. He rolled over and over, down the sloping deck, until he was finally stopped abruptly when his body hit the side of the charthouse. The fall and subsequent tumble severely injured his left leg, but he found that he could stand with difficulty.

The longboat was pulled back and another, stronger line fastened to the stern. Following this, both boats were successfully put in the water. At the very last minute, Captain Barry crawled back to his cabin, entering through a window. He hastily recovered his watch, purse, and a few small personal belongings, which he stuffed in a pocket. Without hurry and with perfect discipline, the men lowered themselves down dangling ropes into the tossing boats. In the tradition of the sea, Captain Barry was the last to slide down one of the lines. The injured mate and four of the sailors took to the jolly boat. All the rest, including the captain, crowded into the much larger longboat.

The first light of the new day was breaking by the time the boats were pushed away from the wreck of the *Oakland*. Dimly at first, then more clearly as the morning light grew stronger, the shipwrecked men saw that they were less than half a mile from land. With oars that had been left securely stowed in the

boats for just such an emergency, they slowly made their way through the towering waves to safety.

When the boats neared shore, the men saw that they were approaching a coast bounded by rocky headlands and cliffs, some of which rose almost straight up out of the sea. A little to the south of the nearest point of land they could discern the entrance to what appeared to be a small cove. When the boats entered the cove, the shipwrecked mariners found that they were in a little horseshoe-shaped bay with a firm sand beach on which they were able to land.

Captain Barry and the crew of the *Oakland* discovered that they had landed near the Welsh village of Rhoscolyn. It was a small agricultural community, nestled in a shallow amphitheater that opened to the south, facing the cove where the men had beached their boats. The hamlet was composed of stone houses and cottages, some of which dated from Elizabethan times and even earlier. Among the cottages were a few excellent examples of the famed Welsh " long house " in which the beds were fastened to the walls, like the berths on a ship. There was a post office and a general store in the center of the village. Separate from the rest, standing in a grove of trees and facing the cove, was a small inn. Behind the village were moorlands and farms. The men had landed on the southern tip of Holy Island, in the county of Anglesey, about five miles as the crow flies from the relatively large town of Holyhead. By carriage road, the distance was somewhat farther.

The villagers of Rhoscolyn came to the immediate aid of the stranded men. They took the sailors from the *Oakland* into their homes, gave them food, dry clothing, and places to sleep. Captain Barry and Thomas Curtis went to the inn to stay.

The twenty-third of March dawned clear and calm. Captain Barry and Thomas Curtis, together with some of the crew, went back to the scene of the wreck in the ship's longboat. They determined that there was much that could be salvaged. Then, in Rhoscolyn, the captain made arrangements for his crew to be housed and boarded for an indefinite period in the homes and

farmhouses of the little town. The men would be paid their regular wages while they salvaged what they could from the *Oakland*.

This attended to, Captain Barry hired a carriage to take him to Holyhead from where he took the stage to Liverpool. In the city, he reported the loss of the *Oakland* to the authorities, then he contacted the Liverpool representative of the *Oakland*'s owners who, in turn, initiated a claim for the payment of the ship's insurance. The captain next arranged for an auction to be held at Rhoscolyn for the sale of whatever materials could be salvaged from the ship. Lastly, he arranged for the eventual passage home for himself and those members of his crew who might wish to return to the United States. They would sail aboard one of the new Cunard steamships, which had commenced service to Halifax and Boston five years earlier, in 1840. Another relatively new steamer and the pioneer of regular trans-atlantic steamship travel, the *Great Western*, was making scheduled sailings from Liverpool to New York, and it was this ship that was then carrying most of the ocean mail between Great Britain and the United States.

On his return to Rhoscolyn on March 26, Captain Barry turned his attention to supervising the salvage of the remains of the *Oakland*. The ship's longboat was used to laboriously bring ashore masts, sails, anchors, chains, and many other items, including ninety bales of wet but salable cotton. It was a prodigious task that was destined to last several weeks.

At the inn, on the night of his return from his hurried trip to Liverpool and for the first time since the afternoon before the wreck, Captain Barry permitted his thoughts to drift in the direction of home. A confirmed bachelor for many years, whose only love was the sea, he had finally met a girl he could not resist. She was Sarah Cleaves Lord, the attractive and then twenty-four-year old daughter of William Lord, a businessman and shipowner of Kennebunk, where the *Oakland* had been built. Sarah was a well-educated young woman and the oldest of nine children in one of the leading families in the community where she lived. As her mother, who was also named Sarah, was not well, Sarah had the responsibility for raising and caring for the younger members of the Lord family.

Captain Barry was particularly distressed over the loss of the *Oakland*, because the ship had played a major role in his romance with Sarah Lord. It had been the *Oakland*'s launching that had first brought him to Kennebunk and it was on the deck of the *Oakland*, the day he took command of the ship, that he had first met this pretty girl with long dark hair and sparkling brown eyes who was now his fiancée. Since that memorable day in May 1841, the love that had blossomed between Charles Barry and Sarah Lord had had much to do with the ship. In time, the captain and Sarah had become engaged and now they were planning to be married in June. As it was now late in March with a great deal to be done before he could sail for home, there was not much time to spare before Captain Barry's wedding date.

These were the days before the telegraph had come into use, Samuel F. B. Morse having made his first public demonstration of electric telegraphy only the previous year, in 1844, and it would be twenty-one more years before the first successful transatlantic cable would be laid. The only way to communicate over any distance of consequence was by letter. Sarah Lord and the others in Kennebunk and Boston who were interested would not learn of the fate that had befallen Captain Barry and his ship for another three weeks. The captain therefore had many letters to write, but he understandably chose to address his first thoughts to his beloved Sarah. By the light of a candle at a small desk in his room at the inn at Rhoscolyn he wrote that night as follows:

Caernarvon Bay
March 26, 1845

My dear, dear Sarah,

How happy I am to be able to write you, and I know that you have long been anxiously looking for a letter from me. I regret, dear Sarah, that I cannot write you a letter that would cause you happiness. But it is so, my love, and I must tell you that misfortune has visited me. I have lost the *Oakland*, the good ship that has carried me safely over so many miles of ocean. It occurred on the morning of March 22nd, at 2:15 A.M. while running for Holyhead Light during a very strong southwest gale and rather thick weather. We went on some very dangerous rocks about five miles from Holyhead, and the ship became a total wreck. The second officer and one man were drowned, and there was some injury to the first officer but he has now fully recovered.

I am well and in perfect health. I have so many papers and documents to get ready to send to Liverpool to go by the *Great Western* that I can write you only a few hasty lines. I cannot go into the details of the *Oakland's* loss in this letter, but when I get home, sitting by your side or in your arms' embrace, then will I relate all the occurrences of the accident.

Oh, I know how badly you will feel, dear Sarah, at this news, but do not let it make you unhappy. No blame can be attached to me, and, though I have met with misfortune, I am not depressed or cast down. The energies of my character are still left and I do not fear that my character will be injured. I do not know that you will dare trust to blend your future with mine and may fear that the anxieties which I create for you will be more than the happiness I can ever repay. But, no, that could not be you. I know you better than that, and misfortune only binds me more closely to you. If you could fear to be mine now that I have met with disaster, I would grant your wish to be free, and then go myself, I should not care whither.

In the midst of the shipwreck and all its trials, I thought of you, and after I had done all in my power for the ship, and expected to save only my life, I crept into one of the cabin windows, took my watch and purse with gold in it, and the ring which I bought in remembrance of you. I had your dear letters, which I had been reading, in my hand but I knew it was useless to try to save them. I put them back and got out of the window. . . . .
Still try and love me, dear Sarah, in spite of my misfortunes, and be assured that my heart's affections can never be other than thine.

Adieu, love, for the present. One kiss.

Ever and truly, your Charles

During the days that followed, the damaged cotton from the *Oakland* was shipped on wagons to Liverpool, where it was sold for the best price obtainable. The auction of salvaged material from the ship was not held until the seventh of May. As the things that were salvaged piled up on shore, it was necessary to hire a watchman. The auction, which lasted five days, brought a fleeting moment of excitement and prosperity to the little village of Rhoscolyn. The records showed later that the topmast studding sail brought five pounds, British currency. The list

was a long one. The ship's windlass, as an example, went for three pounds, five shillings; a cabin chair was worth five shillings, sixpence; and the *Oakland*'s longboat that had done such valiant service after the wreck was sold for six pounds. Two shillings, fourpence had been spent for " powder and shot for the watchman."

Just before he sailed for Boston on the Cunard paddle-wheel type steamship, the *Britannia,* early in June, Captain Barry received a letter which bore the most heartening news he had heard since the wreck. His older brother Samuel, who was then in business in New York, wrote:

Dear Chub,
    I have just received your letter per the *Great Western* and am happy that you have about finished your old ship. I was pleased to learn when in Boston a few days ago that you were completely exonerated from all blame by the insurance officers. I suppose that now you will soon be off to Kennebunk to be married. . . . .

THE BARRY COAT OF ARMS

Arms: argen, three bars, gemels, gules
Crest: out of a castle with two towers, argent, a wolf's head, sable
Motto: *Boutez en avant*

I

The Making of a Sea Captain

From the time of the American Revolution, Brookline, Massachusetts, has been one of Boston's most fashionable suburbs. In the early 1800's it was one of the little cordon of towns that surrounded the Bay State's capitol city with a peaceful environ of green, well-kept lawns, tall trees, and spacious homes. The pattern was broken here and there by ponds, open meadows, and wooded hillsides. Most of the homes were provided with a combination carriage house and stable that was attached either at the rear or the side of the house. Some of the families living in the town even kept one or two cows for fresh milk, and a few had a pig or two. The only traffic along the unpaved streets in the residential area of Brookline consisted of carriages drawn by spirited, well-bred horses, delivery wagons, and people on foot.

Sitting some distance back from the street behind a row of elm trees that provided a heavy shade, one of these homes in early nineteenth century Brookline was a large square-framed house whose distinctive features would today be known as colonial architecture. The place was the residence of Samuel Barry (1761-1835), and it was here that his son, Charles Edward Barry, was born on January 15, 1811. Samuel Barry was a hatter by trade who owned and operated a small but prosperous men's hat

factory in Watertown, a few miles northwest of Brookline. He
also maintained a retail hat store in downtown Boston on
Washington Street. As a young man, Samuel had been a member of a large family of very moderate means that had moved
to Milton, Massachusetts, from Boston when the British took
possession of Boston during the Revolution. Samuel had started
his own hat business at the age of twenty-one. His only asset in
the beginning had been a bundle of furs so small that he could
carry it tied up in a large handkerchief. By the time Charles
was born, he had amassed a comfortable fortune.

Charles Edward Barry's mother (1772-1835) came from one
of Brookline's most respected families. Before she married
Samuel in the First Parish Church of Brookline on November 3,
1802, she had been Rebecca Marshall, the daughter of the wealthy
William Marshall who had made his money as an importer of
English goods prior to the Revolution. An energetic, almost
tiny woman, Rebecca was a true aristocrat who saw to it that
her family upheld the highest standards of social etiquette and
gracious living of that day. " She was a real Christian," Captain
Barry said of her in a letter he wrote after her death. " Her
hand was ever extended to the needy and she often watched at
the bedside of the sick." Rebecca Barry was also a good mother
who performed her duties to her children faithfully. " She
instilled in our minds those principles which, if followed, will
cause anyone to be respected, let their station in life be what
it may," wrote Captain Barry.

Charles Barry himself was one of six children. He had two
older brothers, Samuel and John, and three younger sisters, Mary,
Rebecca, and Abigail. Mary died while still in her teens and
John died shortly after he was married, when a relatively young
man. Charles's sister Rebecca was nearest to his own age. She
had been born in 1813 and was named for her mother. Of all
his brothers and sisters, Charles loved Rebecca the most.

There was one other member in the family of Samuel Barry.
Rebecca, his wife, had had an older sister Mary, who had married
a man named Curtis. These were the days before the miracles
of modern medical science, and people seldom lived as long as

they do today. Both Rebecca's sister Mary and Mary's husband died very early in life, leaving an orphaned daughter named Maria. After the death of her parents, Samuel and Rebecca Barry adopted young Maria Curtis and raised her as one of their own. Although she was older than they were, the Barry children always regarded her as a sister. When she grew up, she married Thomas Curtis, the successful merchant and shipowner of Summer Street, Boston, for whom Captain Barry later sailed. Although his last name was the same, Thomas Curtis was no relation to Maria.

Charles Barry attended the best private schools during his youth in Brookline and grew up as a healthy, typical New England boy. Like most of the boys of the period who had been born along the coast, he had a touch of the sea in his blood, which was natural because the entire economy of the area depended upon maritime shipping for its livelihood. The railroads had not been built and the center of activity of every coastal city and town was at the waterfront. The youthful Charles and the other boys of his neighborhood never missed an opportunity to cross the Charles River and visit Gray's Wharf at nearby Charlestown. In complete fascination, they would watch as colored stevedores, chanting as they worked, unloaded strange and exotic cargoes from tall-masted sailing ships that had arrived from ports all over the world. Though the lads of Charles Barry's group were not aware of it at the time, the fleet they so often saw being unloaded was manned, for the most part, by successive waves of adventure-seeking Yankee boys in their late teens and twenties who had obeyed the call of the deep blue water. The officers had come from those among them who had determined to make the sea their calling.

The favorite topics when boys gather today are automobiles and airplanes. In knowledgeable terms, they debate the relative merits of American-made and foreign cars and they speak of reciprocating, jet, and turbofan engines, the take-off thrust of a turboprop, carburetors, fuel injection, and compression ratio. In Charles Barry's day, boys talked of barks and brigantines, ships and topsail schooners. And they knew precisely what they were

talking about when they spoke of a futtock, apron, timber strake, treenail, stemson, keelson, mizzen, spanker or jib boom.

It is not hard to imagine what thoughts ran through the mind of young Charles as he and his playmates watched the ships being unloaded at Charlestown. All of those lovely ships at the wharf with their tall, tapering masts, slim sides, and marvelously carved figureheads seemed to possess a knowledge of the many places to which they had sailed. What a multitude of romantic visions must have been conjured up in the minds of the boys just by the enticing smells of the ships! An endless series of dreams came, no doubt, as they whiffed the odor of Stockholm tar, coffee from the West Indies, wool from Australia or South America, copra from Tahiti, jute from Calcutta, and spices from the Orient. Or they might have pictured Valparaiso or one of the other nitrate ports of the west coast of South America with a roadstead crowded with the flags of many nations, all waiting to take on their cargoes.

As Charles grew older, he found that even his school curriculum had a nautical flavor. His Greenleaf's *National Arithmetic* had sections devoted to customhouse business, reduction of currencies, tare and tret, tonnage and gauging. Geography was a living subject. The inadequate description of foreign countries and their ports found in the textbooks came alive when it was supplemented by the graphic accounts given by friends of his father and men in the neighborhood to whom Liverpool, Shanghai, Capetown, Le Havre, New Orleans, and the ports of the West Indies were as familiar as their own backyard. Hardly an hour of any day passed that Charles, as a boy, was not in some way reminded of sailing ships. There were but few boys who could grow up near the New England coast in the early 1800's and resist the lure of the sea.

The way of life of people all over the world had not changed very much for more than a hundred years when Charles Barry was born. At the start of the nineteenth century the industrialization that has remade the face of the earth and completely changed all of man's social habits had barely begun. But in the course of Charles Barry's lifetime, great technological advances

that affected the everyday lives of everyone were destined to take place. The availability of the new commodities that manufacture in mechanized factories made possible, the coming of the railroads, and the start of world-wide steamship service were exciting events. They were, in fact, as exciting and as far reaching in their effect in Charles Barry's day as the advent of radio and television, the universal use of automobiles, and fast around-the-world transportation in modern jet airliners have been during the twentieth century. The changes that were to take place between the early 1800's, when Charles Barry was born, and the 1850 period, when he died, started slowly at first, then, as man acquired mechanical know-how, gained momentum rapidly.

Although an Englishman named John Kay had invented the " flying shuttle " in 1733 to lighten a weaver's work and multiply his output, it was not for another thirty-five years that such men as John Hargreaves, Richard Arkwright, and Samuel Crompton commenced making successive improvements in the spinning of cotton to meet the weaver's insistent calls for more, stronger, and finer yarn. When Arkwright patented a machine to spin yarn by water power in 1769, the factory age and the start of the industrial revolution that was to change the world's standard of living was at hand.

A few years after Arkwright started to use water power for spinning yarn, James Watt and Mathew Boulton worked the bugs out of a contraption run by steam that Thomas Newcomen had invented in England in 1702. By 1777 Watt and Boulton had developed the first factory steam engine. They used it to operate the machinery in the ironworks owned by a man named John Wilkinson. It worked so well that Richard Arkwright began using steam power for spinning, and in the early 1800's looms operated by steam power were invented for weaving cloth in factories. These developments multiplied the productivity of individual textile workers more than a hundred-fold, and the industrial revolution was on.

The first successful American factory was set up by Samuel Slater in 1791 to spin cotton for merchants in Providence, Rhode Island. The little mill had seventy-two spindles tended by nine

children under the supervision of a factory overseer. Their
wages ranged from twelve to twenty-five cents a day. By the
War of 1812, when Charles Barry was just one year old, hundreds
of factories like Slater's were at work. Most of them were in
New England and they were operated by men that Slater had
trained.

Under the management of these men, who knew little about
keeping accounts, handling labor, and developing markets, many
of the early mills were wiped out by the financial panic that
followed the War of 1812. But along with the early mechaniza-
tion of the textile industry had come advances in machine design, improvements in metal working, and most important of all,
the development of the principle of interchangeable parts for
the machines themselves. The American cotton textile industry
survived the postwar financial collapse, and the advances that
had been made in the infant art of building power-driven machines gave impetus to the construction of more and better mills.
So-called " new model " factories of improved design sprang up
and commenced to flourish under new leadership. The first of
these factories was opened at Waltham, Massachusetts, in 1816.
Called the Boston Manufacturing Company, the business had
been incorporated three years earlier by Francis Cabot Lowell,
Patrick Tracy Jackson, Nathan Appleton, and other men of the
same caliber. The group, who called themselves the " Boston
Associates," built the first wholly integrated cotton manufacturing plant in the world, with all operations under one roof, and
they set up their own selling agencies.

The Boston Manufacturing Company was an instant success.
Its operation at Waltham set the pattern for other enterprises.
The younger and more farsighted businessmen of the area were
quick to put their money and brains into making eastern New
England an important manufacturing center. Every country
town with a good-sized stream set up a textile or paper mill,
an ironworks, a shoemaking factory, or a cordage plant. And
the same vision and energy that made eastern Massachusetts,
southern New Hampshire, and coastal Maine into a great work-
shop also served to increase the maritime activity along the New

England coast, particularly at Boston, which was the hub of the new industry. Manufacturing stimulated the import of wool from Australia and South America, of coal by ship from Philadelphia, and of cotton from the Gulf ports and South Carolina and Georgia. The new textile plants also provided a new American export commodity — domestic cotton fabrics, which Yankee vessels introduced into the world's markets.

The end of the War of 1812 marked the end of a forty-year period of wartime conditions and foreign interference in American living. The post-bellum inflation that followed the war was liquidated in 1819. The year of 1820 was an important one, for it marked the beginning of a toilsome advance in the economy of the New England coast. Later came a speeding up of trade and manufacturing, in the 1830's, with full-scale prosperity arriving during the 1840's. The concentration of industry and the population in the larger cities of the eastern seaboard that came with industrialization called for mass transportation of raw materials from distant points and of finished products to faraway markets. Between 1820 and the late 1850's New England maritime commerce increased approximately 800 per cent. And it was in 1820 that Maine became a separate state and no longer a district of Massachusetts. With the advent of the steam-powered sawmill in 1820, a period of great activity commenced in the lumber business along the New England coast. From this time on, the logger, the river man, the sorting boom, and the spring logging drive became an integral part of the economic picture.

By the time Charles Barry was a teenage boy in Brookline, every tidewater village between northern Maine and Long Island Sound had a packet sailing sloop, schooner, or brig plying the waters between its home port and Boston or New York. As an example, the town of Plymouth, Massachusetts, had a population of less than five thousand in 1830, yet six sloops of sixty tons each were required to handle the trade between Plymouth and Boston. They exchanged local products for raw materials used in Plymouth's textile, iron, and cordage factories. Two schooners of ninety tons each plied around Cape Cod to Nantucket, New Bedford, and New York.

There was a similar lively coastal trade by packets that sailed regularly between the cities and towns of the entire Atlantic seaboard. The plentiful lumber from northern coastal towns was shipped to southern cities, whose local supplies of lumber had been exhausted. The ships returned with cotton for the New England textile mills. The cotton carrying trade had expanded rapidly after the invention of the cotton gin by Eli Whitney in 1793, which enabled the cultivation of short staple cotton to be undertaken. At such ports as New Orleans, Mobile, Savannah, and Charleston, the available supply of cotton more than doubled between 1820 and 1830.

The wharves at Boston became the transfer point for the re-shipment of goods to the smaller New England towns. Busy coastal traffic was supplemented by the arrival and departure of ships that traded regularly with the West Indies. For the most part, these vessels exchanged New England lumber for rum, coffee, and molasses at such places as Cuba, St. Croix, Jamaica, and the Dutch ports. Coffee was the most preferred return cargo because of its small bulk in relation to its value. In addition, a never-ending procession of square-rigged ocean-going sailing ships brought goods to the city's wharves from French and British ports, the Mediterranean and the Baltic, South America, the East Indies, and the south seas. By 1830 an average of eight coastal vessels and three or more ships from foreign ports were arriving at Boston every day. The number greatly increased during the decade that followed.

Boston at this time was growing by leaps and bounds. Between 1820 and 1830 the population increased from forty-three thousand to sixty-three thousand. The effect was felt throughout the suburbs as the hustle and bustle of everyday living increased in tempo. This apparently did not suit Samuel Barry at all, for about 1825, he moved his family from Brookline to Watertown, ostensibly to be nearer to his hat manufacturing business. But any business advantage that he may have gained by the move was short lived. In 1827 he suffered a stroke that

paralyzed the left side of his body. He was a complete invalid for the rest of his life. "All his business was brought to a close," wrote Captain Charles Barry later. "Our family continued to live happily at Watertown with the exception of my father's affliction," he said.

Charles Barry was sixteen years old at the time of his father's stroke. Shortly afterward he took a job at his father's former retail hat store on Washington Street in Boston. But the call of the sea was far too deeply imbedded in his make-up by this time for him ever to be contented with such routine work as selling hats. He soon left the hat store to work as an apprentice in a merchant's counting room that was, in effect, a bookkeeping office on Central Wharf on the Boston waterfront.

The bulk of the overseas trading of the period was conducted by merchants who owned fleets of vessels, both large and small. These men traded with many countries on their own account, they chartered their ships to others, or they took freight for others when the opportunity offered. They distributed their cargoes on arrival at Boston by auction sales held in rooms on the wharf or through their own stores, which were located either in the city or on the wharf. All of the many transactions were accounted for in counting rooms such as the one in which Charles Barry, at seventeen, took employment.

Central Wharf had been built in 1819 as a companion to India Wharf, which had been constructed several years earlier. On Central Wharf there were fifty-four stores for handling imported goods in a long brick building that ran down the center of the wharf for a quarter of a mile. On the upper floor of this great building were three huge halls for auction sales of incoming cargoes. In an octagonal cupola on top of the building was the headquarters of the Semaphore Telegraph Company to which the approach of arriving ships was signaled as soon as a ship was sighted by a lookout on nearby Telegraph Hill. The telegraph company, in turn, notified whomever might be concerned that such-and-such a vessel had just entered the port. In the stores on the first floor of the long brick structure were the display rooms, the warehouses, and the counting rooms of many of Boston's leading mercantile firms. As on India Wharf, it was here that cargoes from all parts of the world were brought, sold, and accounted for without the aid of clacking typewriters, adding and tabulating machines, or an established office system.

In the counting room Charles Barry sat on a high stool, along with other male clerks who made entries with a pen in longhand on the pages of calf-bound books and ledgers. From time to time Charles would have to get down from his stool to delve into one of the neat wooden chests in which the records of some particular vessel were kept. The air in the room was strong with the pungent aroma of tar and hemp, mingled with the spicy odors of the East Indian and Oriental goods that were stored in an adjacent warehouse.

Through the small-paned windows of the counting room in which Charles worked one could see the masts, spars, cordage, and half-loosened sails of the ships that were tied up at the dock. When a cargo of coffee or molasses came alongside the wharf or when lumber was being loaded, the air resounded with the songs of the Negro stevedores. They hoisted hogsheads out of the hold of a ship with a block and tackle, singing as they worked. There were no winches in those days, and when these were later introduced, the Negroes disappeared from the Boston wharves. They claimed that they could not sing above the noise the winches made, so they no longer applied for work as stevedores.

A gauger stood on the wharf as the cargo came out of a hold, checking the hogsheads and boxes against the ship's manifest. Since this document occasionally failed to list all the cargo, there sometimes arose the problem of getting the surplus off the ship and into the warehouse without its being detected by the customs inspector. In such cases the problem was sometimes solved by the ship's owner taking the inspector home to dinner and lingering long over the wine. When they belatedly returned to the wharf, the excess goods would have already been hoisted out and stored in a warehouse without appearing on the counting sheet.

Working in the counting room on Central Wharf only served

to intensify the call of the sea as far as Charles Barry was concerned. In October 1829, at the age of nineteen, after two years
in the counting room, he took the inevitable step by signing on
as an apprentice boy aboard the *James Perkins* under the command of a Captain Crowell.

The *James Perkins* was a three-masted ship with square sails
on all masts. She was about 450 tons in size, with the usual
black hull and white waist that was so typical of that period.
The vessel had been named for a prominent Boston merchant
who was a partner of the famous mercantile firm of J. & T. H.
Perkins, which owned the ship. James Perkins himself and his
even better-known brother, Thomas Handasyd Perkins, were
scions of a wealthy family of Boston pioneers. It had been
James Perkins who in 1821 had attained a local immortality of
sorts when he gave his new and beautiful home on Pearl Street
to the Boston Athenaeum. The Athenaeum made the house its
headquarters until permanent quarters were built on Beacon
Street in 1849.

The many months that Charles had spent in the counting
room had not been wasted. Unless a ship's master carried a
supercargo in those days, he had to be a skilled trader as well
as a competent commander of his ship. When in port, it was
the captain's responsibility to dispose of his cargo at the best
available price. He often had a financial interest in his vessel,
but whether he did or not, it was up to him to see that the
vessel made money for the owners. After selling his outgoing
cargo, a captain had to shop around, bargain, and close the deal
for the cargo he would either carry home or take to some other
port. Often he had to lay at anchor in a foreign harbor for
weeks while waiting for a profitable cargo to become available.
A supercargo, when there was one, was a passenger aboard the
ship who represented the vessel's owners as business manager,
thus relieving the captain from this task. He worked only when
the ship was in port and had no duties at sea. But only a few

of the old square-riggers carried a supercargo, all of the financial details being normally handled by the captain. It was a responsibility that required self-reliance and a sound knowledge of world commerce and economics. The two years that Charles Barry had spent in the counting room had provided the best business training he could have had for the master's job that lay ahead.

In the days of square-rigged ships, boys and young men of sea-captain caliber were apprenticed to the seafaring trade for training in ships at sea. There was no such thing as an established school where deserving aspirants could be taught to be officers in the merchant marine. The only way that an American youth could learn to command a sailing ship was by on-the-job training under the direct tutelage of a qualified shipmaster. Apprentices had to work their way up from the forecastle by learning to be able seamen, and good ones at that, before there was any selection for promotion up through the grades of second, then first mate, and on to the command of a ship of their own. It was a long, hard road to travel, although on occasion, the road was made somewhat easier and shorter through family influence. When this was the case, it was called " coming in through the stern windows."

Charles Barry sailed aboard the *James Perkins* for nearly seven years. At the end of the first two, he attained his rating as an able seaman, and his pay was raised from eight to twelve dollars a month. The standard of seamanship had never been higher than it was at that time. Charles, as an apprentice, had had to become an expert at splicing, seizing, parceling, gaffing, pointing, worming, and serving, all of which was a part of the art of rigging. He had been taught to reef and to steer, to reeve all the studding sail gear, set a topgallant and a royal studding sail out of the top, to loosen and furl the royal or flying jib, and to set down, or cross, a royal yard. Constant hard work was the rule, as Captain Crowell was a fair but stern master when it came to training his crew.

Seafaring, at best, was a rough and dangerous calling. Much heavy and hazardous work had to be done aloft in the complex

rigging. The spars were heavy and awkward to handle; the sails were difficult and tricky to set or trim. To set a main topsail, for example, required the handling of eleven different lines simultaneously. On dark nights sailors had to be able instantly to use an almost unbelievable amount of gear — and use it correctly — without being able to see what they were doing. The rig of a ship with single topsails, like the *James Perkins,* consisted of nine mast pieces, two bowsprit pieces, twelve yards, two gaffs, twenty sails and one hundred and twenty-six parts of standing rigging that had to be set up and in good condition. There were over two hundred running ropes, almost three thousand pounds of gear in ties and sheets, three hundred and thirty-five single pulley blocks, eighty-three double blocks, two treble blocks, a hundred and twelve deadeyes and a hundred and eighty belaying pins. All of these parts and many others had to be kept in perfect order and free from chafe. Working a square-rigged sailing ship was a task that required all the art of an able seaman. A good captain had to know everything that there was to know about every bit and piece of his vessel's intricate gear, and more. It required a lot of hard work and training before a man could be qualified to become a ship's master. Captain Barry wrote later that there were many times during his early years at sea when he wished he were back in the counting room, but his perseverance and determination would not let him turn back once he had made up his mind what he wanted to be.

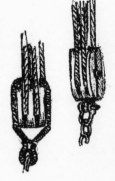

After his apprentice training was over on the *James Perkins,* Charles Barry served as seaman, second mate, first mate, and finally as master, all under the watchful eye and guiding hand of Captain Crowell. When Charles was promoted to the position of master, Captain Crowell continued to sail on the ship as a supercargo. The *James Perkins,* for the most part, freighted sugar from Batavia to Amsterdam, and in 1835, a voyage was made to India. After rounding the Cape of Good Hope on her return, the ship encountered a violent storm and her cargo shifted, necessitating that the vessel be put in at the island of St. Helena to trim cargo.

The *James Perkins* with Charles Barry now her captain arrived at Boston during March 1836 at the end of the India voyage. To his sorrow, Captain Barry learned that both his father and mother had died during his long absence. Samuel Barry had passed away on January 20, 1835, as a result of his prolonged illness, and Rebecca had followed him to the grave just ten months later, on November 9, 1835. Almost equally distressing to Captain Barry was the news that his favorite and beloved sister Rebecca, who had been teaching at a girls' seminary at Taunton, Massachusetts, had been taken seriously ill. On the invitation of Mrs. Harriet Strong, a cousin, she had moved to Rochester, New York, where she hoped to be able to rest. Harriet and her husband, William Strong, were wealthy. They had offered to share their home with Rebecca in the belief that they could nurse her back to health.

When Captain Barry's older brother Samuel (who was known in the Barry family by his middle name, Frederick) settled the estate of their parents while Charles was still on the India voyage, he invested the money from Charles's share of their inheritance in South Boston real estate. The property did not increase in value and the money was eventually lost. Samuel, who had married Martha Lewis Peabody of Salem, Massachusetts, later failed in business in Boston during the financial panic of 1837. He moved to New York City where he started in all over again with the firm of Whitwell, Bond and Company, who were importers of wool. In time, he became a rich man.

Within a month of his return in the spring of 1836, Captain Barry left, once more, to again sail the *James Perkins* to India with Captain Crowell as a supercargo. The round trip to Bombay and back required the better part of a year. This time, the saddest news of all was awaiting Charles when he docked his ship at the wharf in Boston. Rebecca had died at her cousin's home in Rochester, on July 13, 1836.

Charles's youngest sister, Abigail, whom the family called "Abby," had gone to Rochester to help the dying Rebecca. There she met a Mr. Clarendon Morse whom she married in the fall of 1837. But in less than two years and soon after the birth of her first child, Abby herself became sick. Quite suddenly, she too died in Rochester. The date was May 27, 1839. Of the six children of Samuel and Rebecca Barry, only Charles and his brother Samuel were left, and in 1838 Samuel had moved to New York. After that, and except for his cousin Maria, Charles had no immediate family living within two hundred miles of Boston.

Upon reaching Boston in the spring of 1837, at the end of his second voyage to India, Captain Barry left the *James Perkins* to remain ashore for several months. It was to be his longest vacation since he had first commenced working in the counting room on Central Wharf nearly nine years earlier. He was now twenty-six and felt that the time had arrived when his social contacts should be renewed after his long absence from the Boston and Brookline society in which he had been reared. He was an active man who enjoyed good company, dancing, and other interests. Years later, one of the men who had at one time served as first mate on one of Captain Barry's ships said of him, " He was an admirable character who was always very neat about his dress, often wearing gloves. He attended carefully to business and was always lively and witty in his conversation." And after his death, Captain Barry's wife described him when she wrote:

> He was a gentleman in every respect. He was well-bred, intelligent, bright and lively. He did not appear like a man who was cut off from society for months at a time, and he was very domestic in his tastes and habits. Everybody liked him.

Early in 1837, just a short time before Captain Barry arrived from India, a new hotel was opened in Boston at the foot of Lincoln Street. Named the United States Hotel, it was the largest and one of the finest in America up to that time. On leaving the *James Perkins,* Captain Barry engaged a permanent room at the new hotel, which he thereafter made his home whenever he was in Boston.

The United States Hotel made an ideal bachelor residence for a seafaring man, and its dignity and prestige provided a background befitting an East India sea captain. As the hotel was within easy walking distance of India, Central, and Long Wharves, it was the gathering and stopping place for many another ship's master. And it was only a few minutes' stroll from the hotel, up Lincoln Street, to Summer Street, where many of Captain Barry's friends, including Thomas and Maria Curtis, had their homes.

Having made two voyages to British East India, Charles now belonged to the exclusive fraternity of elite East India merchants and shipmasters. Prior to the Civil War, East India men, as they were called, were several notches higher up the social ladder than anyone else in the seafaring trade, no matter what the position of the others might be. There was even a remark, often made about a pretty girl from an exceptionally good family in those days, that went, "She's good enough to marry an East India captain." Charles Barry, with his poise, erect bearing, good manners, composure, and the aggressiveness that went with his small stature fitted the part perfectly.

By 1837 Boston had changed greatly from the city that Charles had known when he was a lad of sixteen, working in his father's former hat store on Washington Street. Not only had the effects of the mechanical evolution started to make Boston and the surrounding area into a manufacturing center, but the arrival of steam power was commencing to bring about other miracles, not the least of which were steamships and the railroads.

One of the surprises that Captain Barry received upon his return to this country was to see a railroad in operation. There had been talk about railroads ever since the first railway passengers in the world had been carried on the crude Stockton and Darlington line in England in 1825. But to actually observe a steam locomotive pulling a train of cars in his own home city of Boston was something for which the captain had not been prepared. It was such a captivating spectacle that Charles found,

as others had, that he could not resist going to the railway terminal, whenever he could, to marvel each time a train arrived.

A railway, actually, was nothing new to the Boston area. As early as 1826 three miles of wooden rails protected by strap-iron plates had been laid on stone sleepers from a granite quarry at Quincy down a slight grade to water level on the banks of the Neponset River. The cost of the project was fifty thousand dollars, and its purpose was to move the granite blocks that were being used to construct the Bunker Hill Monument. Once the granite reached the river, it was transported by water to Charlestown where the monument was being built. From the quarry, the traffic over the rails was all downhill, so single horses could easily pull heavy loads, the only problems being to keep the loaded cars from going too fast and to get the empty ones back up the hill again. This was the first American railroad and it was operated — always by horsepower — for about forty years.

The first steam-powered railroad in the United States had been built at Charleston, South Carolina, where a group of men engaged Horatio Allen to get a railroad going. Allen had laid six miles of rails in the direction of Savannah and he had had a locomotive built in New York City. The locomotive was hoisted aboard the rails at Charleston in December 1830, to pull the first train of cars ever moved by steam in this country.

The success of the South Carolina Railroad brought a rash of incorporations of other proposed rail lines in all the settled regions of the United States. A passenger train of the Mohawk and Hudson Railroad was put into operation between Albany and Schenectady in October 1831, and in 1832 the Baltimore and Ohio Railroad put on a steam locomotive to replace the horses it had been using to pull coaches between Baltimore and Endicott Mill. At the same time, the rails of the Baltimore and Ohio were extended to Frederick, a total distance of almost fifty miles. In New England, the Boston and Worcester, the Boston and Lowell, and the Boston and Providence Railroads were all granted charters in 1830. But it was not until nearly five years later that all three of these lines approached completion almost simultaneously.

The first locomotive to run in New England was imported from England. It was set in motion on the tracks of the Boston and Worcester Railroad during the latter part of March 1834. By April it was hard at work pulling a gravel train over nine miles of track between Boston and Newton. By 1835 all three of the new rail lines were in full operation. That they were successful from the beginning is indicated by the receipts of the Boston and Lowell Railroad, which took in sixty-five thousand dollars the first year. In 1836 the receipts on this line were a hundred and sixty-four thousand dollars, and the Boston and Worcester line was transporting about a hundred passengers daily by the following year.

The terminal for the Boston and Worcester Railroad was built on reclaimed land that had once been South Cove, not far from the United States Hotel where Captain Barry had gone to live. The engines and rolling stock on this and other railroads were naturally quite primitive at first—neither very safe nor very efficient. The first locomotives, all of which were too early to be used on the Boston roads, had come in highly varied designs, some with upright boilers and some with their boilers mounted horizontally. The crew of both types rode standing up, out in the open, exposed to the weather, sparks, and smoke. The tender was a stubby flat car on which a hogshead of water and a pile of wood were carried. The first railroad coaches for passengers were in the familiar form of a stagecoach, just as seventy years later the first automobiles were built along the lines of a horse-drawn buggy. The stagecoach-type passenger cars proved dangerously top-heavy and were soon discarded.

When the three Boston roads commenced operation in 1835, railroad equipment had improved to the point that engines had started to take on the present classic shape of all steam locomotives, even though the first engine cabs were nothing more than canvas stretched over a wooden frame. The boilers were horizontal, and a large funnel-shaped smokestack was at the front. By 1837, when Captain Barry saw them, the passenger cars on the Boston roads were oval-topped, box-like affairs with side windows. They were entered from the ends, as are the cars on American railroads to this day. A long, hard wooden bench ran the length of the car along each side, from front to rear. The cars had four pairs of wheels, but no springs, and they were coupled together by a very unsatisfactory link and pin arrangement. As a result, the bucking and jerking when a train started up or came to a stop was terrific. The trains themselves were called a " brigade of cars" and to ride on one was known as "taking the cars." By modern standards, neither the Boston and Worcester, the Boston and Lowell, nor the Boston and Providence was much of a railroad, but at the time they represented the ultimate in traveling luxury even though their top speed was seldom in excess of twenty miles an hour.

The railroads represented only one phase of the changes that were taking place in the field of transportation in early 1837. Wherever seamen gathered and with whomever Captain Barry talked that spring, one topic more than any other inevitably entered the conversation. Although it would be another year before steamships in regular service would commence crossing the Atlantic, paddle-wheel type steamers had been in use on American inland waterways for more than a decade, and it was now known that a man named Isambard Brunel was building a very large steamship in England, which, he predicted, would "obsolete every sailing ship in the world." The inland steamers had not caused much concern to sailing ship men because they were both small and awkward and could only ply the rivers where plenty of wood was always available to keep their boilers going.

But steamships on the Atlantic in regular service was something else again. Most seamen of the day simply didn't believe in steam power. To smut-up clean sails and to go against the wind was heresy to old sea dogs, to say nothing of what the competition of steam would mean to the sailing ship trade. The fathers of these men had enjoyed a good laugh when an Irish gunsmith from Pennsylvania, Robert Fulton, had imported one of James Watt's steam engines from Birmingham, England, and had put it in his ship the *Claremont* to steam up the Hudson River from New York to Albany in thirty-two hours during 1807.

And no one had paid very much attention when the experimental auxiliary steamer *Savannah* had sailed from the city for which she was named to Europe in 1819.

At first, the steamers relied on conventional sails for most of their power and used their steam-driven paddle wheels only as an auxiliary. The first Atlantic crossing by steam power alone is uncertain, although there is no doubt that by 1837 the Atlantic had been crossed at least three times by ships that had been much more dependent on their steam engines than on their sails. The ships involved were the *Curacao,* the *Radmanthis* and the *Royal William.* All had probably used sails when the wind was favorable. The hulls of these vessels were similar to sailing ships and their rig, while much lighter than that of a sailing vessel, was sufficient to bring them into port in the event their machinery failed. When they were under sail, it was customary to remove a few paddle wheel blades from each side paddle, then turn the wheels until the submerged portion was the section from which the blades had been removed. Thus blades did not drag in the water and hold the ship back when she was being driven by sail.

Speculation by Captain Barry and others about what effect steamships might have in the future soon gave way to a much more real and immediate concern over quite another matter. Between 1820 and 1837 investment in American industry had risen from fifty to two hundred and fifty million dollars. By 1837 bank notes and discounts reached the then unheard of total of six hundred and seventy-five million, most of this representing advances in the price of land that had been forced sky-high by the new settlement in the cities, the progress and promise of better transportation, and the speculative fervor which these factors had spawned. As always under such conditions, debt rose faster than the ability to pay, and the inevitable day of reckoning finally arrived. In June 1837 a financial panic descended upon the American economy. But although a worldwide depression followed and lasted until 1839, the crash of 1837 only put a slight dent in the progress that industrialization and shipping were making. Boom times were just around the corner.

About the only effect the financial crisis of 1837 had on Captain Barry was to prolong his vacation ashore longer than he had planned. The curtailment of shipping during the depression threw many shipmasters temporarily out of work while ships without cargo lay idle in Boston Harbor. Charles Barry remained in that city during the winter of 1837-38.

There were many things to keep an idle shipmaster busy in town that winter. If one were a member of the Merchants Club or Topliff's News Room, as Captain Barry was, these were excellent places to pass the better part of almost every day. The center of mercantile and municipal Boston at the time was the Old State House at the head of State Street. Built in 1748 to house the government of the Province of Massachusetts, its walls had once resounded to the eloquence of John and John Quincy Adams. After the state government moved to Beacon Hill, the Old State House became the Town Hall, and subsequently, the City Hall. In 1837-38 the three-story, one hundred and ten by thirty-eight foot building housed not only the municipal government of Boston but the Post Office and the Merchants Club, as well. And under the alderman's chamber, looking down State Street, was Topliff's News Room, a subscription club and reading room for Boston merchants and sea captains, when the latter were in port. Newspapers and periodicals from all parts of the world, a complete register of the entrances and clearances of vessels in American and foreign ports, and bulletins from foreign correspondents all over the world were kept on file. After a Merchant's Exchange Building was built on State Street in 1842, Topliff's News Room moved to that location and the Old State House was given over to shops and offices.

Another of Captain Barry's favorite places to visit that winter was the home of Thomas and Maria Curtis on Summer Street. All of his adult life, whenever he was in Boston, he had made it a point to spend every Sunday afternoon with the Curtises. This particular winter, he spent a great deal more time than usual with them. Summer Street, which is a continuation of Winter Street, was then the favorite residence of many prominent merchants, shipowners, and retired Boston businessmen. The Curtis home was one of the provincial Federal mansions that were surrounded by gardens and great elm trees along each side of the street. The first shop invaded Summer Street in 1847, and by the Civil War the section was wholly given over to business.

For evening entertainment, there were many private balls given in the city that fall and winter by Captain Barry's friends. These were crowded, brilliant affairs where there was cotillion dancing for the young, cards and conversation for the old, and for those who loved to eat, an excellent buffet of fine food and wines. There were also little cotillion parties at someone's home almost every weekend, and there was the theater, which was attended regularly by almost everyone who was anyone in Boston society, including Captain Barry.

The captain enjoyed himself immensely during the entire period he was ashore. He was invited everywhere, and wherever he went he was immensely popular, socially. Boston society matrons with marriageable daughters considered him the bachelor catch of the season. Before she died, his sister Rebecca had worried about what was to become of him and once she had written to him in this manner:

> I wonder if you will ever marry, Chub. How amusing it would be to see you parading about with a bride hanging on your arm. What kind of a woman will you choose? I can't think of one in my whole circle of acquaintances that might serve. Well, time will reveal the secret. Perhaps your heart will center in the little foot of a Chinese damsel, or you may be carried captive by some little French flirt, with eyes as roguish as your own . . . . .

But through it all and in spite of the fact that many a clever trap was laid to capture his heart, the head of Captain Charles Barry remained unturned.

II

Ice and the Bark Madagascar

Three years before Captain Barry spent the winter of 1837-38 on shore at Boston, an event took place in South America that was destined to have an indirect effect upon his future. One day late in 1834, the bark *Madagascar*, six weeks out of Boston, sailed into the harbor of Rio de Janeiro. For her period, she was a relatively large three-masted vessel with square sails rigged on yards on her two forward masts. There was a large fore-and-aft sail on the after, or mizzen, mast. The time was about the middle of the morning on a scorching hot day. The sailors working on deck and in the rigging perspired freely as the bark hove to and dropped anchor. But hot weather was normal for this time of year, as this was the beginning of summer in Brazil.

As soon as the formalities of entering the port and declaring the ship's cargo with the Brazilian customs officials were over, the supercargo from the *Madagascar*, a man named Osgood Carney, announced that he was giving a party aboard the ship that night. As guests, he invited a number of city and government officials. When issuing the invitations, Carney hinted that a pleasant surprise would be in store for those who came.

At the appointed hour, the guests were met at the wharf, then taken in small boats to where the *Madagascar* lay at anchor. Each visitor was greeted by Osgood Carney as he came aboard. Then he was asked what he would like to drink. Some wanted

tea or coffee, others preferred wine, and of course, a great majority said they would like a drink of something much stronger, such as whiskey or rum, perhaps, if these were available. To their great astonishment when the steward brought their orders, the men discovered that their drinks were ice-cold. They were even more amazed when they found that their glasses actually tinkled with chips of real ice that had been placed in the drinks. It was the first ice and these were the first cold drinks that had ever been seen in Rio de Janeiro. As a refreshment on such a hot night, the drinks were a treat that had never been equaled before in that part of the world.

In reply to his visitors' many excited questions, Carney ordered one of the bark's hatches opened. By candle light, he showed his guests the cargo. The *Madagascar* had brought one hundred and eighty tons of ice in two-hundred-pound blocks all the way from Boston. The Brazilians could hardy believe their ears when they were told that only a very little of the ice had been lost by melting because the vessel's holds had been double sheathed and the ice had been packed in sawdust. The hatches had been kept tightly sealed to prevent melting during the long voyage.

Osgood Carney explained that the ice belonged to Frederick Tudor of Boston, who had been exporting ice to southern climates for more than twenty years. Tudor had, in fact, successfully shipped a consignment of ice all the way from Boston to Calcutta — a voyage which required four months — only the year before. He now wanted to extend his ice trade to South America, this being an experimental cargo. A suitable storage house would be needed immediately, which would require government cooperation. In return, Tudor would agree to deliver ice to Brazil regularly provided he could be assured of an exclusive ten-year monopoly.

Before the party aboard the *Madagascar* broke up that evening, the guests were served ice cream that had been made from fresh cream brought aboard the ship that afternoon. It was the first ice cream that most of the Brazilians had ever tasted. Later, as his guests took their leave, Carney arranged for a

meeting with them and others for the first thing the following morning.

The man for whom Osgood Carney worked, Frederick Tudor, had been born in Boston on September 4, 1783, the day after the treaty that brought the American Revolutionary War to a close was signed at Paris. Tudor had turned down a chance to attend Harvard and had elected, instead, to pursue a business career that commenced when he was only thirteen years old. In 1805, according to legend, he was approached at a party by a friend who jokingly suggested to Tudor that he commence exporting the winter ice from his father's pond at Saugus, Massachusetts. But the then twenty-two-year-old Tudor did not take the remark as a joke. He became so convinced that the idea had possibilities that he bought the brig *Favorite,* which he outfitted to carry ice. He had heard of the ravages being made in the West Indies by yellow fever, which was sweeping whole towns and villages. Ice would lessen the terror if it were available. During the winter of 1805-6, Tudor sent the *Favorite* to Martinique with an experimental shipment of a hundred and thirty tons of ice taken from the pond at Saugus.

The ship's crew at first refused to sail with the ice, saying that it would melt and swamp the vessel, but with some difficulty, they were persuaded to make the voyage. Frederick Tudor sent his brother William and his cousin, John Savage, ahead to pave the way and receive the ice when it arrived at Martinique. It was sold to individuals in small quantities and used to reduce the fever of yellow fever victims, to make ice cream and cool drinks, and to preserve foods and medicines. Although the Martinique venture lost money, it did show that ice could be transported over long distances to a warm climate. Nevertheless, Tudor's early efforts seemed pure folly to most Boston businessmen and though George Washington, Thomas Jefferson, and James Monroe had all harvested and stored ice, his friends thought him mad. "We hope this will not prove a slippery speculation," one Boston newspaper had quipped.

The following year, in 1807, Tudor shipped a cargo of ice to Cuba in the brig *Trident.* Again, he lost a great deal of money. Through the early years of his attempts to create a foreign market for New England ice, he was hounded by one failure after another, yet his belief and determination remained undaunted. By the time he had built an ice storage house at Havana and started to attain limited success in 1816, he had been in and out of debtor's jail in Boston and he had been "pursued by sheriffs to the very wharf." He extended his business to Jamaica, and between 1817 and 1820 he commenced operations at Charleston, Savannah, and New Orleans. Thereafter, Tudor's ice brigs and schooners were a common sight in the southern ports of the United States and in the West Indies. From the hundred and thirty tons that he shipped in 1806, Frederick Tudor's exports of New England ice jumped to four thousand tons in 1826 and sixty-five thousand tons by 1846. By the latter date Tudor owned ice houses all over the world. He obtained ice from nine main sources around Boston, which included ponds in Cambridge, Arlington, Ayer, Woburn, Wakefield, Andover, Lynnfield, and Wenham. Later, ice also came from the Kennebec and Penobscot Rivers in Maine.

The New England ice export business eventually put millions of dollars into the pockets of farmers, merchants, and shipowners from Boston to the northern shores of Maine. In every New England village with a pond near tidewater, the harvest of ice became the farmer's surest crop.

Tudor's story was one of pain, perseverance and ingenuity. Not only did he have to create his own markets, but no one in the southern ports knew how to use ice or how to store it during hot weather. Tudor had to teach local bartenders how to employ ice without wasting it when mixing drinks, and coffeehouse owners had to be shown how to make ice cream. He had to provide the materials for icehouses, hire builders to construct them, and set up a sales organization to handle and sell the ice once it reached its destination. "The best method of carrying ice in small quantity is to wrap it in a blanket. These may be had at the icehouse of a sufficient size at $1." read a Tudor advertisement in a Charleston, South Carolina, newspaper. To carry ice in his ships, Tudor experimented with all types of dunnage. He tried packing the ice in rice and wheat chaff, hay, tanbark, and even coal dust before he finally discovered that ordinary pine sawdust made the best packing material and insulator.

What Frederick Tudor was up against and how he established his business at a new port is well illustrated by the instructions he gave his supercargo, Osgood Carney, before the *Madagascar* left Boston with the first shipment of ice for Rio de Janeiro:

> If you can make a commencement for introducing the habit of cold drinks at the same price as warm drinks at the ordinary drinking places, even if you have to give the ice, you will do well. The shop frequented by the lowest people is the one to be chosen for this purpose. You must promote an ice cream establishment, instruct people in the art of preserving ice at their homes, construct a temporary ice house on shore, introduce it to hospitals and persuade the Brazilian government on the grounds of public health to remit export duties on all products taken away by the Tudor vessels.

Osgood Carney accomplished his mission with diplomatic expediency, and another foreign capital was added to the growing list of Tudor ports of call. After the *Madagascar* was thoroughly cleaned and dried out, she returned to Boston with a cargo of Brazilian coffee.

The *Madagascar* was owned by Captain Barry's friend Thomas Curtis, who had leased the vessel to Frederick Tudor for use in his ice trade. Tudor crews continued to operate the bark for the remainder of 1834 and through the years 1835 and 1836. After the volume of his business dropped during the depression that followed the panic of June 1837, Tudor returned the vessel to Curtis. The *Madagascar* lay idle in Boston Harbor, along with many other ships, during the fall and winter of 1837-38.

But meanwhile, crews of men were busy out on the ice ponds of eastern Massachusetts. From December until early March,

whenever the ice was thick enough, they harvested the winter crop and stored it away for shipment the following summer. At Fresh Pond in Cambridge, across the Charles River from Brookline, the ice had attained a thickness of fourteen inches early in February. One Monday morning, a group of Irish laborers under the direction of Frederick Tudor's ice-harvesting expert, Nathaniel J. Wyeth, arrived at the pond with ice-cutting tools and a number of horses harnessed with bridles and reins, collars, hames, and traces. Not long afterward, sleigh bells could be heard coming up the road. A single-seat sleigh drawn by a sleek chestnut mare drew up by the icehouse, close to the edge of the pond. After tossing aside the buffalo robe that covered their legs, Thomas Curtis and Captain Charles Barry stepped out. Curtis tied the horse to a convenient hitching post, then threw a blanket over his back. The two men walked to the edge of the pond to watch the ice-cutting operation.

The crew first used shovels and horse-drawn scrapers to remove several inches of snow from the ice on the pond. Then a man riding what resembled a small sled pulled by a single horse traveled up and down the length of the pond. The sled had vertical iron runners with saw-toothed edges that etched deep parallel lines in the ice, about eighteen inches apart. The next step was to cross these lines at ninety degrees with other lines, roughly three feet apart, that were cut by a grooving tool. The groover, which was also pulled by a horse, was equipped with plow-type handles and a marking device that scratched a line to indicate where the next line should be made. As in many of the other operations, two men were required, one to lead the horse and the other to guide the machine, much as a farmer would plow a field. Soon the ice resembled a giant checker board.

Next, sawyers with one-man, double-handle ice saws cut down the length of two of the eighteen-inch parallel lines for a distance of several hundred feet. The first blocks of ice nearest the shore were broken loose and lifted from the surface of the pond by hand. After this, the sawyers cut fifty-foot strips of ice, one at a time, which were pried loose to float in the open water. These were pushed with gaffs toward the icehouse. A wooden

conveyor chute had been assembled in sections and run from an open door in the side of the icehouse to the water. A giant of a man armed with a spade-ended crowbar stood by the lower end of the chute. As one of the fifty-foot strips floated past him, he thrust heavy, repeated blows at the ice. Every time his crowbar fell, a two-hundred-pound block broke loose along one of the marked cross-lines.

As it broke away, each block was caught by tongs in the hands of men standing on the ice close by. They eased it to the bottom of the chute where another man attached a pair of tongs that were fastened to the end of a rope that ran up the chute and over a pulley to where a horse was standing nearby. The rope was tied to the whiffletree, or swinging bar to which the traces that ran from the hames of the horse's collar were fastened. At the cry of " Ho!" from one of the men at the chute, the driver of the horse slapped his reins, clucked to the animal, and guided him as he pulled the block of ice to the top of the chute. Here the block was transferred to another chute and pushed into the icehouse, where it was stowed away. As each layer of ice was laid, it was covered with several inches of sawdust. The process went on endlessly. The dark forms of the men and horses contrasted sharply with the glistening blocks of ice. Their breath steamed in the crisp, cold air. The scene resounded with the shouts of the men as they bantered back and forth among themselves in the give and take of their work.

On the way back to Boston, Thomas Curtis turned to Captain Barry. Speaking loud enough to be heard above the jingle of the sleigh bells, he said, " How would you like to take a cargo of that ice we just saw to South Carolina next month, Chub?"

" Very much, although I'd like to know more details," the captain replied.

" Last fall when the price was down, I bought several hundred bales of cotton in a warehouse at Charleston," said Curtis. " I now have a buyer in Antwerp. Fred Tudor wants to ship a consignment of ice to Charleston in March in the *Madagascar*.

SHIPS LOADING ICE AT TUDOR WHARF, CHARLESTOWN, MASS.

Rather than continue to lease Gray's Wharf, Frederick Tudor bought the wharf shortly after Captain Barry's time, changing the name to his own. The scene in this later-day photograph is undoubtedly much the same as when Captain Barry took on ice here in the ship *Delhi* during December 1846.

Photo courtesy The Peabody Museum, Salem, Mass.

I want you to hire a crew and make the voyage to Charleston and from there to Antwerp for me." After thinking it over a few minutes, Captain Barry agreed to sail the *Madagascar* for Thomas Curtis that year.

The first week in March saw the bark tied up at Gray's Wharf at Charlestown, which had been built by the shipping magnate and one-time Lieutenant Governor of Massachusetts, William Gray (1750-1825). Although Frederick Tudor later bought the wharf and changed its name to Tudor Wharf, he now only had it under lease for his ice export operation. Spring was late this year and snow still covered the ground. In the icehouse at Fresh Pond workmen pried loose the stored blocks of ice by means of chisels, then loaded them on horse-drawn pungs. These arrived at the wharf one after the other in a long procession that pulled up beside the *Madagascar*.

A hand-operated machine had been set up on the deck of the ship. This consisted of a horizontal windlass with two gigs, or small platforms, that went up and down on tracks between the wharf and the deck of the ship by means of a cable wound around the drum of the windlass. While one of the gigs at wharf level was being loaded with ice from one of the pungs, the other was on the deck of the ship being unloaded. As one gig went up its track, the other came down. Once on deck, the blocks of ice were sent down a chute through an open hatch. In the hold of the ship, men packed the ice away and covered each layer with sawdust. As only about three hundred tons of ice could be loaded in a day in this manner, it required about a week for the vessel to take on her cargo. Captain Barry took her down the harbor and out into Massachusetts Bay on his way to Charleston about the middle of March.

The *Madagascar* was still at Charleston, loading Thomas Curtis's cotton, when news arrived that a transatlantic race that would go down in history as one of the greatest maritime events of the century had terminated at New York. The date was April 23, 1838. Since that day, the maritime world has continually vied for a mythical blue ribbon that is said to belong to the merchant vessel holding the record for the fastest time across the North Atlantic.

The transatlantic race in April 1838 marked the beginning of a new era in ocean travel. The initial phase of this event had commenced two years earlier, on July 28, 1836, when the keel of the greatest vessel up to that time was laid down in England. This was the pioneer transatlantic steamship *Great Western*. She was the product of the fertile imagination of Isambard Kingdom Brunel, a young British engineer who had already won fame for his vision and daring. Upon the completion of his brilliant work as chief engineer for the Great Western Railway when their railroad was built from London to Bristol, Brunel had said, half jokingly, " Let me extend the line to New York by building a steamship to run across the Atlantic."

Brunel's idea was discussed further, the outcome being that he was told to go ahead and build the vessel he had in mind. She was a wooden ship of especially heavy construction, two hundred and twelve feet long, thirty-five feet in beam, and twenty-three feet in depth of hold. A paddle-wheel type steamer of one thousand three hundred forty tons, the ship had a two-cylinder, jet-condensing, side-lever engine that developed seven hundred fifty horsepower. Steam pressure from rectangular boilers with internal fire boxes and flues was a maximum of about fifteen pounds per square inch. The use of sea water in the boilers necessitated the wasteful practice of blowing them down at regular intervals, replacing the hot water lost in this manner with cold sea water to reduce the brine concentration. The *Great Western* carried her passengers and officers in the after part of the ship, leaving the more desirable mid-section available for the machinery. The crew's quarters were forward.

About the time that construction was started on the *Great Western,* the British and American Steam Navigation Company was founded to operate a line of steam packets between British ports and New York. The first vessel built was the *British Queen,* whose overall length was two hundred seventy-five feet. The failure of the contractor for her side-lever paddle-wheel engine to deliver it on time delayed the ship's completion. The owners

of the *British Queen* therefore decided to charter another steamer to commence transatlantic service ahead of their rival, the Great Western Company. The vessel selected was the little channel packet *Sirus,* whose length was only two hundred feet. Her two-cylinder side-lever engine was unusual in that it was fitted with a surface condenser and the vessel used fresh water, not sea water, in her boilers.

The *Sirus* left London on March 28, 1838. She put in at Cork for fuel and finally departed for New York on the fourth of April. The *Great Western,* in the meantime, was delayed en route from London to Bristol by a fire and did not sail for New York from the latter port until the eighth of April. The little *Sirus* had a rough passage. At one time her crew commenced to mutiny and demanded that her commander, Lieutenant Roberts of the Royal Navy, turn back. But Roberts would not. The ship reached New York at 10:00 P.M. on the twenty-second of April. Her crossing had consumed eighteen and a half days.

The record of the *Sirus* did not stand for more than a few hours. Early in the morning of the twenty-third of April, after a passage of only fifteen days and ten hours, the *Great Western,* with seven cabin passengers, steamed into New York Harbor. Her average speed was 8.6 knots and she had consumed 655 tons of coal. The success and speed of the voyage of both the *Sirus* and the *Great Western* ended for good the years of debate that had transpired over the practicability of a transatlantic steamship service. From this time on, steamers sailed regularly between England and the United States.

Captain Barry's voyage from Boston to Charleston with Tudor's ice, thence to Antwerp with cotton for Curtis, and the return to Boston required most of the remaining months of 1838. Unable to obtain a cargo at Antwerp, he had had to sail in ballast to Liverpool where he purchased a shipload of mixed British manufactured goods, which consisted mostly of woolens.

Upon his return to the United States, Captain Barry learned that Thomas Curtis had ordered a ship to be built in the shipyard of Henry Kingsbury at Kennebunk, Maine. The vessel, which was being designed primarily for the cotton-carrying trade,

would be named the *Oakland*. Curtis offered Captain Barry the command of his new ship. But, Curtis explained, the *Oakland* would not be ready until early in 1841, as her lines had not even been laid down. Captain Barry was elated and promptly accepted the offer. It was agreed between the two men that he would continue as master of the *Madagascar,* sailing for Curtis until the *Oakland* was ready.

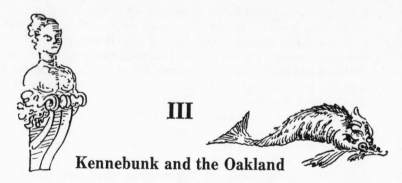

III

Kennebunk and the Oakland

On arriving at Boston from a European voyage in March 1841, the *Madagascar* was met at the wharf by her owner.

"I have just closed a deal to sell the *Madagascar*," Curtis told Captain Barry, "but the *Oakland* will be launched at Kennebunk in just a few weeks. You can go down to Maine at any time and wait there to receive her."

Most New Englanders today think of Maine as "up" from Boston because it lies to the north, or "up" on the map, from Massachusetts. When sailing ships were the principal mode of travel along the coast, Maine was "down" from Boston because one sailed with, or down, the prevailing southwest wind to reach it.

By 1841 the Eastern Railroad had commenced to operate trains from its terminus at East Boston to Portsmouth, New Hampshire, which was the end of the line. The part of this railroad that ran between Newburyport and Portsmouth had been opened for regular travel about mid-November 1840. But the line from Portland, Maine, to Portsmouth via Dover, which was being built by the Portland, Saco and Portsmouth Railroad Company to meet the Eastern Railroad at Portsmouth, had not been extended south of the town of Saco. Captain Barry therefore elected to travel by stagecoach when he journeyed from Boston to Kennebunk in April.

By the old stagecoach road, the distance was roughly a hundred miles, which is considerably longer than it is along U.S. Route One today. In the stagecoach days, which drew to a close not long after the last link of the Boston-Portland rail line was completed in 1842, the post road between Boston and Portland was marked by large granite stones at one-mile intervals that had been erected on the order of George Washington when the Colonial Post was started. Two types of stage, both operated by the Portland Stage Company, traversed this road. One was the mail coach, carrying mail and six passengers on an express schedule seven days a week. The other was the slower accommodation stage, which carried nine passengers six times a week and made an overnight stop at Portsmouth, where the passengers had to obtain rooms at an inn.

Captain Barry took the speedy mail coach that traveled all night. It made the fastest possible time in order to reach Portland by 10:00 A.M. with the Boston newspapers of the day before. The fare to Kennebunk was six dollars. The trip to that point required seven changes of horses and twelve hours travel time.

After an early supper in Boston, the captain boarded the stage at 7:00 P.M. The vehicle was a standard Concord coach of the type that had been invented by Lewis Downing of Concord, New Hampshire, in 1815. It was a picturesque affair, ornately painted in yellow and gold, and drawn by two pair of matched black horses. Whale-oil side lamps cast a dim light ahead that would not have done much good if the horses had not been thoroughly familiar with the road.

When it was new, the coach had cost over two thousand dollars, no small amount at the time. The driver, like the others of his calling, wore new store clothes in preference to the more familiar homespun. He was arrayed in a fancy tailored overcoat, fur hat, and gloves. On the highway he had the unquestioned right of way over all other vehicles, and no matter how tamely he permitted his horses to trot or walk outside of town, he always arrived with a great deal of dash and spirit at a scheduled tavern stop. The sound of his coachman's horn was familiar throughout the countryside. On approaching an inn, the number of toots he blew on his horn would signal the land-lord how many passengers he would have to feed.

On arriving at Kennebunk, about 7:00 A.M., the coach was met by Isaac Hilton, landlord of The Hilton House, local head-quarters of The Portland Stage Company. As many as sixty horses were kept in stables at the rear of the inn. Sufficient horses were maintained fully harnessed, in readiness to be quickly hitched to any stage the moment it arrived. The hostler slept in the tavern barroom so he could hear the clatter of horses' hooves on the flagstones of the spacious courtyard whenever a guest drove up or a stage arrived during the night.

" Hilton's," as the tavern was known, was the friendly meet-ing place of the businessmen, doctors, lawyers, and shipbuilders of Kennebunk. Spirits were sold as a matter of course, the estab-lished price being five cents a drink, with a spoonful of molasses added to sweeten the toddy.

A hearty breakfast was served to the passengers on the 7:00 A.M. stage before the coach, now drawn by fresh horses, departed for Portland, leaving Capain Barry behind. He en-gaged a room at The Hilton House, then unpacked his carpet-bag, shaved, and changed his clothes. His first order of business that day was to walk by himself around Kennebunk to see what the town was like, as he had never been there before.

Kennebunk, Maine, is unique in that it is the only town in the world by this name. The word is of Indian origin and has been said to be formed by joining three words of the abo-riginal language: " ken," signifying " long "; " neb," signifying " water at rest "; and " unk," meaning " land " or " place." Putting these words together, the resulting name means a place where there is a long stretch of water at rest, which applies to the lower part of the Kennebunk River by which the town is bounded on the east.

The township embraces a number of settlements with a pro-fusion of names that are nearly the same. Inland, three miles from the ocean, is Kennebunk Village, which is the primary town. The Mousam River whose mouth is near Kennebunk Beach flows along the west side of Kennebunk Village. To the

MAIN STREET – KENNEBUNK

Looking west along Main Street in Kennebunk Village during the 1860-1880 period. The Hilton House (or Hilton's) where the first son of Captain Barry was born can be seen on Tavern Hill at the left center of the photograph. This famous inn was originally known as Jefferd's Tavern and, in 1861, it was re-named the Mousam House. It was probably around that time that the columned porch and piazza were added.

Photo courtesy The Brick Store Museum

east is the Kennebunk River, which is the outlet of Kennebunk Pond, situated in the town of Lyman, about fourteen miles from the town of Kennebunk. The river flows in a south-south-easterly direction through meadows and woodlands until it turns abruptly, doubling upon itself, then it flows between high banks until it reaches Kennebunk Landing, the site of six active ship-building yards in the mid-nineteenth-century period, at one of which the *Oakland* was being built. Not far below Kennebunk Landing, at Kennebunkport, the river reaches the ocean. Nor are these all the Kennebunks, for there is also a West Kennebunk and a Lower Kennebunk Village.

As Captain Barry left The Hilton House to walk around Kennebunk Village on his first morning in town, he noted that the most prominent building on Main Street after he had crossed the bridge over the Mousam River was a three-story brick edifice at the corner of Fletcher Street. There were stores fronting on the street on the lower floor, salesrooms on the second floor, and the meeting hall of a Masonic lodge on the third. The building had been built in 1809, gutted by fire in 1824, then rebuilt, and a wooden, brick-faced annex added, which in Captain Barry's time, was an inn called Mousam House. The proprietor of the inn was Johnathan Stone.

A little farther up Main Street, near the intersection of Summer Street, was another, though smaller, brick building, which dated from 1825 when it had been built by William Lord. Up until the year before Captain Barry first saw the building, William Lord had used the place as a general store where he sold groceries and dry goods. A former sea captain and now a shipowner, he was a moderately well-to-do trader with many interests in and around Kennebunk. He was a man of old New England stock, whose father, Lieutenant Tobias Lord, and grandfather, Captain Tobias Lord, had served in the American Revolutionary War. Since 1840, William Lord had been leasing his brick building to others because he was now too active in shipbuilding and shipping interests to also operate the store.

Approximately across the street from Lord's brick building was the First Congregational Church of Kennebunk, whose frame

had been raised in 1774. Its graceful steeple, which has caused this particular church to become renowned for its beauty and symmetry, was not erected until nearly thirty years later, at which time a Paul Revere bell — the third to be purchased in the District of Maine — was hung in the belfry. The pulpit in the church is somewhat remarkable. The enormous mahogany log from which it was fashioned by local joiners was found drifting in the Gulf of Mexico. As the log was too large to be hauled aboard the Kennebunk ship that found it, it was towed behind the vessel all the way back to Maine.

A unique feature about this particular church is that it is not a Congregational Church at all but Unitarian, which was Captain Barry's religious denominational preference. The Orthodox Congregationalists who had originally built the church had withdrawn in the middle 1820's and built their own church, which is known as the Second Congregational Church of Kennebunk, on Dane Street. A sign on the original church now reads " First Congregational Church of Kennebunk " and under the sign in letters larger than the first appears the word "UNITARIAN." Captain Barry worshipped many times at this large white, attractive church, although he never dreamed that this would come about when he first admired the edifice in April 1841.

The strolling captain turned to the right and proceeded east on Summer Street, which was the street the stage line took when it left Kennebunk on its way to Portland. On either side of the wide gravel road were magnificent homes with expensive fences, gates, large cased posts, and division fences between the lots. Young elm trees lined both sides of the street. The large houses were mostly of Georgian architecture. As these were the residences of the town's leading merchants, shipowners, shipbuilders, and retired sea captains, they had been artistically and skillfully built by ship joiners, wood carvers and cabinetmakers brought from the shipyards at Kennebunk Landing. Their attractive line and form was a product of that finest school of design — the marine architects who had perfected their art by modeling some of the world's finest sailing ships.

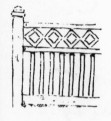

Kennebunk was typical of many other Maine-coast shipping and shipbuilding towns of the period. From Kittery to Eastport, the area had been the scene of seafaring activity for over two hundred years. First, this rugged coast had been a summer fishing ground for English vessels that crossed the Atlantic every season to catch, dry, and carry fish back to Europe. Then the coast of Maine became the eastern border of a vast tract of forest land that for over a hundred years furnished the Royal British Navy with tall pine masts for its ships of war. Although the first pioneers in Maine were fishermen, the principal industry in Maine up to the time of the American Revolution had been cutting, finishing, and shipping these large masts to England. The best of these were over one hundred feet in length, and they measured thirty-six inches in diameter or more at the butt. Hewed and dressed, they were worth up to five hundred dollars apiece delivered at the port, ready for shipment. Masts were cut so they were as many yards long as they were inches in diameter at their base. Their great size required specially built mast ships. These were built in both England and Maine with large ports so they could load their bulky cargo. The ships could carry from fifty to one hundred of the largest masts, together with bowsprits, yards, spars, and other pieces.

After the Revolution struck the death knell to the market of masts for the Royal Navy, the coast of Maine turned to lumbering and shipbuilding. The lumber export business reached major proportions in the first part of the nineteenth century. Coasters and West Indian freighters sailed out of every port in Maine with lumber to trade for cotton, rum, molasses, and coffee. The lumber cargoes varied. Planks, boards, and "deals," which were pieces of timber three-by-nine inches in cross-section that were to be sawed at their destination, were known as "long lumber." Clapboards, laths, fence posts, and bolts of shingles were "short lumber." The long lumber was brought from the mills on great rafts, which were warped or skulled by skillful oarsmen to where a ship lay at the mouth of a river or port. Loading the many vessels that plied the trade went on both day and night.

Shipbuilding in Maine had been going on for over two hundred years. The first ship constructed in America, *The Virginia of Sagadahock,* had been a Maine-built ship, launched in 1607. Subsequently, many a provincial shipbuilder in Maine had laid his keel and built his vessel on a shore surrounded by growing timber from which he cut the lumber for both his ship and its cargo. By the early nineteenth century, hundreds of vessels of varied types were being built along the banks of almost all the rivers in Maine. Prior to the Civil War, the typical shipyard was a small-scale enterprise under the direct supervision of not more than one or two men. During this period, the shipyards of New York and Boston were crowded to capacity with high-class vessels — packets, two-decked passenger ships, and steamboats — while priority in Maine was given to the sturdy freighters of low cost and superior cargo capacity that were in such demand for the cotton carrying trade. Merchants, shippers, and traders such as Thomas Curtis therefore more often than not bought Maine-built ships.

These were often built in the most suprising places, not the least of which were the yards at Kennebunk Landing. The difficulty experienced in warping the vessels downstream to open water once they were launched made the meadow along the banks of the Kennebunk River at Kennebunk Landing seem one of the most unlikely locations at which to find not one, but six busy yards. Yet, from 1800 to 1880, these yards built and launched a total of six hundred and thirty-eight vessels. In 1841 the farthest upstream at the site was the yard of David Little, where only small vessels were built. Next came the yard of George W. Bourne and Henry Kingsbury, which the two men operated in partnership though each built his own vessels, independent of the other, when occasion demanded. The *Oakland,* which Henry Kingsbury was building himself, was typical of this arrangement. The other Kennebunk yards at this time were owned and operated by George and Ivory Lord, James and George Titcomb, Asa M. Durrell, and Clement Littlefield.

When Captain Barry met with Henry Kingsbury in the afternoon of the captain's first day at Kennebunk, arrangements were

made for them to go together to Kennebunk Landing the following morning to see the *Oakland* and the yard where she was being built. Early Wednesday, Kingsbury picked Charles Barry up at Hilton's from where they drove to the Landing in Kingsbury's carriage. On the way, Kingsbury explained to Captain Barry that most of the lumber for the vessels being built in the yard was hauled from a long distance up in the country during the winter months, on sleds pulled by teams of oxen. Oak timber came from Lebanon, twenty-five miles from the yard. Trunnels, or treenails, of oak and locust wood for fastenings, spars, pine masts, and other wood came from Waterboro and Alfred, which were twenty miles away. The teams would arrive at the yard as early as four o'clock in the morning. The shouting of the men to one another usually awakened the whole neighborhood. Each sled carried feed for its cattle and food for the driver. At times food for the men was frozen so solid that it had to be broken up with a hatchet. On the first good day after one particular spell of bad weather during the previous winter, Kingsbury told Captain Barry, nearly two hundred teams of oxen had arrived at about the same time. They had blocked the road for nearly a mile and temporarily prevented the stage with the mail for Portland from getting through.

On reaching the yard Henry Kingsbury showed Captain Barry where the timber had been piled close to the road as it had been unloaded from the sleds during the winter. Close by was a warehouse building where shipmaster supplies were stored. On a bank stood a building seventy feet long and open on one side, like a lean-to, where the men could work in bad weather. There was a large drafting room in the loft of the building. This was the mold loft where George Bourne and Henry Kingsbury personally laid down the lines of their ships. A clock was in the gable of the building and a belfry and bell were on the roof. At the west end of the structure was a shed where copper, bolts, and other supplies were stored.

A saw pit was beneath this building and another was on the brow of the hill. A third was near the river. These were pits deep in the ground, thirty feet long and four feet wide.

FORMER SHIPBUILDING WORKS, KENNEBUNK-LANDING; & SHIPS AVON, 948 T., AND ALAMEDA, 935 T., UNDER CONSTRUCTION, AUG., 1860. RESTORED BY WM. E. BARRY, ARCH'T. FROM A PHOTO. OF THE GROUNDS, SKETCHES OF THE PRINCIPAL BLDGS., NOW REMOVED TO OTHER SITES, & A COMPLETE PLAN OF THE PREMISES BY GEO. B. LITTLEFIELD, SHIPWRIGHT. (2510)

Ways and rollers were across the top of each. A fourth pit was made from a platform protruding out from a bank, its end supported by posts. When a pit was in use, a stick of timber would be rolled out over it, on which a workman stood to operate one end of a large whipsaw. A second man worked down in the pit, pulling on the other end of the saw. A cloth covered part of his face to keep the sawdust out of his eyes. Together, these men cut and trimmed the timber or sawed it into planks and boards.

There were two shipways in the yard. On one stood the *Oakland*. On the other, the keel had recently been laid for a small schooner that George Bourne was building. The ways had been constructed by first imbedding a row of logs about forty

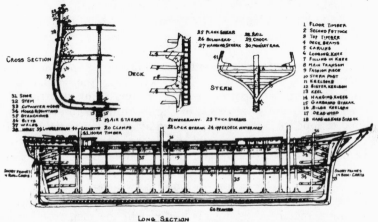

feet long in the ground, parallel to the edge of the Kennebunk River. These were the bed logs that the ways rested upon. The exposed tops of the logs had been faired smooth so the pine boards forming the ways could be placed across and on top of them in the maner of railroad tracks. The ways, on which a ship rested while it was being built, sloped at the proper angle down to the water in the river. At the water's edge, they passed through cribs, called slips. These, in effect, were boxes built of logs that had been filled with stone and earth.

There was a small shop near the river where ship's wheels were made, and another where figureheads and stem boards were carved. In a steam building were two kettles holding several buckets of water, brought up the hill from the river in pails by a small boy who attended the steam box and kept the fire going. He received twenty-five cents a day. An hour was required to steam a plank. Of the two kettles, only one was kept boiling. The water in the other was only heated enough to keep it hot. This was used to replace the water in the boiling kettle without cooling it.

To build the *Oakland,* a total of about thirty men were employed. Among these were master carpenters, carpenters, painters who made their own paint and pigment, fasteners, caulkers, a spar maker, a " tin knocker," and laborers who carried and sorted the timber and planks. Three boys, including the lad who operated the steam box, did various odd jobs about the yard. Most of the men could, and did, perform all or many of the specialized operations that went with building a ship. The pay of these men was small and their hours were long, the regular work day being from sunup to sundown. Strong drink was thought a necessity in the shipyards. In the morning, before the day's work commenced, the men gathered in the lean-to of the big work building where they were served their " portion," this consisting of one glass of rum and two of water. Sometimes " long sweetening," or molasses, was added. This mixture was known as blackstrap. The ration, or portion, was repeated at eleven in the morning and again at four in the afternoon. On special occasions, the cry of " Grog, Ho!" brought the men together to celebrate the raising of a stem or stern post, the hanging of an anchor, or the fastening of the last plank on a ship. A prohibition movement in the Maine shipyards brought this practice to an end about 1850, after which coffee was substituted for rum.

When Captain Barry first saw the *Oakland,* the caulkers had almost completed their work. This was a slow job that had required several weeks. With their irons and long-headed mallets, they forced oakum into the seams between the planks on the sides of the ship. The seams would then be payed over

with melted tar. The *Oakland*'s deck had already been laid, caulked, and payed with pitch. Carpenters were building the hatch covers and doing the finishing work in the forecastle and the master's cabin, while other men were installing the pumps, rails, and windlasses. Everything would be completed before the vessel was launched, except stepping the masts and installing the rudder. These items were not added to ships built at the Kennebunk yards until they reached deep water at Kennebunkport.

Kingsbury explained how the *Oakland* had been built. First, he and Thomas Curtis had conferred together to determine the vessel's size, design, and cost; then a half-model of the hull had been carefully carved by hand. This had been of the type called a lift model, which consisted of smooth boards built up in layers and arranged so the model could be readily taken apart. When he was ready, Kingsbury had disassembled the model so that each layer could be used individually to secure an offset contour of the vessel at each waterline without the use of plans.

From each separate layer of the model, using a compass, square, straight edge, chalk line, and battens, Kingsbury had taken off the lines of the ship and laid them down on the mold loft floor. It had been a difficult job and an important one. In this manner, he had drawn full-size plans of the *Oakland*'s frames, backbone, timbers, deck beams, stern, and sternpost with chalk on the large board floor of the mold loft. From these, full-size patterns had been made from light pine boards. When they were ready, workmen took the patterns to shape each piece of the ship.

Next, the various parts of the ship — the keel and false keel, the frames, sternpost, stern, bow cants, bilge stringers, and so on — had been cut and laid or fastened in place. When the skeleton of the *Oakland* had been ready, the work had shifted to the outside of the hull. As the work progressed, the men in the yard had been divided into specialized groups. There were the hewers, who used adzes to shape the timbers; the sawyers, who cut the frame timbers and planks in the saw pits; the dubbers with adzes, who faired the outside edges of the frames before the planking, or skin, was put on; the borers, who drilled

holes for the fastenings; the liners, who marked the shape and position of each plank; the trunnelers, who made the fastenings — locust wood for the trunnels used below and oak for above the waterline; the fasteners, who drove home and wedged the trunnels by means of heavy mauls; and the joiners, who planed and smoothed the outside and the inside of the vessel.

Only the most rugged men in the yard whose eyes were as quick as their hands did the planking. It was hard, heavy work. Often the plank had to be softened in the steam box. The cry of "hot plank" would bring men running from all over the yard to draw the steaming wood from the box and rush it on their shoulders up an inclined plane to the side of the ship. With the aid of every mechanical purchase available, the plank would be forced tight against the frames, where it was permanently secured by the fasteners who drove the trunnels home.

The iron work for the Bourne and Kingsbury yard was done at a smithshop across the road from the yard by a man whose name, ironically, was S. Jones Smith. Chain, copper fastenings and sheathing, canvas and sails, had to be ordered from outside vendors, some of whom were as far away as Portland. Also in Portland were the shops of the pump and block makers and a mill for picking oakum. A boatmaker in Kennebunk fashioned the *Oakland*'s small boats. S. Jones Smith made the anchors, capstans, and windlasses. The hemp lines for the rigging were manufactured at a rope walk at Kennebunkport.

The rigging of the *Oakland* would not be done until after the ship was launched, at which time Captain Barry, as her master, would be on hand to see that the job was carried out properly. This and many other details were discussed by the captain and Henry Kingsbury as they drove back to The Hilton House that Wednesday afternoon. During the days that followed, Captain Barry visited the shipyard many times to acquaint himself with every intricate detail of the new ship.

On the first Sunday after he arrived at Kennebunk, Captain Barry caught his first glimpse of the girl who would shortly capture his heart. That morning, he walked to the First Congregational Church, across the street from William Lord's store,

to attend the service. On the way, he stopped to speak with Henry Kingsbury. When an attractive young woman brushed past the two men on her way to church, Charles Barry was so impressed with her appearance that he later mentioned the incident in a letter to her:

> How well do I remember the morning I stood talking with Kingsbury when he stepped aside to let you pass. I inquired your name. He said it was a Miss Lord. I remember that I thought you had a pretty face.

The last week in April and the first week in May passed quickly. Soon it was May 13, 1841, the day set for the launching of the *Oakland*. The day was clear and warm. Although to Kingsbury the launching was all in the day's work, it required a great deal of planning and attention to detail. The morning high tide that day would come a few minutes after eleven o'clock. Long before this, people from all over the area had gathered, as they always did, to see the new ship slide down the ways. The yard of Bourne and Kingsbury was gaily decorated with colored bunting, and ropes had been strung to keep people from getting too close to the vessel.

Half an hour before high tide, Kingsbury's most skillful carpenters went down beneath the *Oakland*'s bottom. Working from the stern toward the bow, in pairs on each side of the ship, they used steel-faced mauls and iron wedges to split out the heavy blocks on which the ship rested. An ominous creak issued forth as the last block was removed. Warned by the sound of crushing timber, the carpenters leaped to safety. The assembled crowd commenced to shout as the *Oakland* — slowly at first, then faster as she gained momentum — slid smoothly down the ways. A young yard worker who was riding on the peak of the bowsprit waved his cap and cheered with the crowd as the ship became waterborne in the Kennebunk River.

After launching, a gondola was placed on each side of the stern of the *Oakland*. These were allowed to partially fill with water, then the holes in their bottom were plugged. A beam was lashed across the stern of the ship, from one gondola to the other. The beam was also fastened to the vessel's rudder post. When the water in the gondolas was bailed out, the *Oakland*'s stern was raised nearly a foot, thus making her passage down the river easier.

When the *Oakland* was ready to be warped downstream by means of long lines from her deck to men on shore, a man named Jesse Towne was her pilot. Warping a vessel down the river to Kennebunkport was a difficult job, partly because the river was so shallow that the ship could only be moved at high tide. It always required four tides, and often many more, to get a ship from Kennebunk Landing to Kennebunkport. Towne had been the river pilot of every large ship built and launched at Kennebunk Landing. He was familiar with every turn of the stream and planned in advance the course he would follow with each individual vessel. He was an excitable man and shouted a tumult of orders in rapid succession. " Pull on the starboard side, boys, or the ship will go to the bottom. Pull hard, boys! Pull all together! There she goes, right into the bank and into the mud. Heave Ho! See if you can start her again," and so on. But in spite of his constant fears, Jesse Towne was a good pilot who never failed to get the vessel down the river without an accident.

The *Oakland* would have to lie tied up to a wharf at Kennebunkport for over a month while her masts were stepped, her rudder put on, and her sails and rigging installed. But before the crews who would do this work took over, the ship was cleaned up and made ready for an inspection by everyone in town who wished to pay her a visit. Word was circulated that Henry Kingsbury and Captain Charles Barry would receive visitors aboard the ship at Kennebunkport on a Monday morning, the third week in May. On this same day, Captain Barry would officially take command of the ship.

On the appointed day, most of the nautically minded citizens of Kennebunk and the surrounding towns came to inspect the *Oakland*. Both active and retired sea captains, shipowners, shippers, businessmen, and just ordinary people who were curious went to Kennebunkport. Among the first to arrive was William

Lord and his daughter Sarah. Captain Barry had met William Lord on several occasions, but he had only seen Sarah at a distance, such as the day she had passed him on the walk in front of the church.

Sarah held her father's arm as they walked up the gangway from the wharf to the deck of the ship. Her long dark hair was parted in the middle and neatly arranged in two buns, one over each ear. Her dark brown eyes sparkled with excitement and interest as she took in the *Oakland*'s every detail. She was about two inches shorter than Captain Barry who, himself, was not tall. Her healthy, rosy cheeks dimpled when she smiled as she and the captain were introduced. Their eyes met when they shook hands. A magic something seemed to pass between them, which they were never able to explain. In some unaccountable manner, they were greatly attracted to each other immediately. Then and there, and for the first time in his life, Charles Barry knew instinctively that here was a girl he wanted to marry. When writing to Sarah many years later, he had this to say about their first meeting:

> I was pleased with you from the time we met on the deck of the *Oakland*. I then felt and thought that there was a sympathy of soul, tastes and habits existing in each of us that I had never seen or felt in any other individual. I thought that it would enable us to live happily in each other's society if it should be our lot to be united to each other. I have not changed my opinion from that Monday morning that you rode down to see the ship.

Captain Barry attentively escorted Sarah Lord about the vessel. Before she and her father departed, he had asked and had been granted permission to call on her at her home on Summer Street in Kennebunk Village. He learned that she was twenty years old, having been born on August 7, 1821, which made her ten years younger than he was. He had not seen her with the other young people around the village because she had to stay home most of the time to help her mother, who was not well. The large Lord family required a great deal of attention, and most of the work fell upon Sarah's capable shoulders.

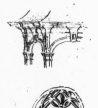

Later that week, Captain Barry accepted an invitation from Sarah to call at the Lord residence for afternoon tea. It proved somewhat of an ordeal, even for one with the *savoir-faire* of Charles Barry. From the youngest to the oldest, each member of the Lord family had to meet and appraise the man who was an obvious candidate to become Sarah's new beau. Sarah's mother, the former Sarah Fairfield Cleaves of the neighboring town of Biddeford, introduced her sister, Mary Cleaves, who was then visiting in Kennebunk. Sarah called her Aunt Mary. And then there were all the Lord children — Sarah's seven brothers — William, Hartley, Robert, George, Daniel, Henry, and Frederick, whose ages ranged from eighteen to three, in that order. Sarah's mother had recently returned from Washington, D. C., where she had spent the winter with another sister, a Mrs. Charles Dummer of that city. Mrs. Lord's poor health made it necessary that she spend the cold winter months in a warmer climate.

The home of William Lord was a very large house on the north side of Summer Street at the top of some high ground called Zion's Hill. The building consisted of two parts. One was the old house, with five bedrooms, low ceilings, and a large farm-type kitchen with a big fireplace and a brick oven for cooking. The structure, which included an adjoining barn, carriage house, and two big woodsheds, had been built in 1756. The new part of the house had been added in 1804. Here the rooms were large and the ceilings high. Although built of wood, the outside walls in this part of the house had an inner lining of brick for added insulation against the winter cold. There was a ballroom and a so-called governor's room for entertaining in the downstairs section and three very large bedrooms upstairs at the head of a winding staircase. Every room in this part of the house was provided with a fireplace and heavy casement windows that could be completely closed off in bad weather by heavy sliding panels built into the casements.

With so many people present, Charles and Sarah had very little opportunity to talk and become acquainted over their tea. But before he left, Charles arranged to drive Sarah, the follow-

ing week, to a place that was then called Mitchell's Mill. Nowadays, the location is a part of West Kennebunk. He would obtain a horse and carriage from the livery stable at The Hilton House. The avowed purpose of this ride was to see the railroad construction work being accomplished in that area by the Portland, Saco and Portsmouth Railroad, which was pushing its way south to Dover, New Hampshire.

When the day came and Charles and Sarah reached the place where the construction gangs were working, so engrossed were they in conversation that they hardly noticed what the men were doing. A hundred immigrant Irish laborers from Boston and dozens of teams of oxen, drawing hand-guided earth scrapers, stoneboats, and wagons, were moving dirt, gravel, and rocks in the process of leveling a bed for the tracks. Oak ties were being laid six feet apart. On top of these, and across them, long white pine sills, eleven inches square, were being placed end to end, in two parallel lines. The ties and the sills were fastened together by treenails, or trunnels, in the same manner that a ship was built. The track was secured to the top of the sills.

Before they left the construction scene, Sarah did explain that Mitchell's Mill had been selected as the site for the Kennebunk depot of the new line. Samuel Mitchell, who had owned the property, had already been promised a job as the first Kennebunk stationmaster. In preparation for the opening of the line, which had been scheduled for early the following year — in February 1842 — Mitchell had commenced building a new home and a general store on the north side of the tracks, near where the depot building was being constructed.

During the ride home, Captain Barry took a turn with the reins around the whipstock on the buggy's dashboard so he would no longer have to hold them in his hands. He allowed the horse to plod slowly, to make the journey back to Kennebunk Village last as long as possible. By the time they arrived at the house on Summer Street, Charles had asked Sarah to marry him. "You'll have to speak to Father," she had replied, adding that although she felt that she might grow to love him, it was all too soon for her to be able to give him her definite answer.

For the remainder of his stay in Kennebunk, Captain Barry called on Sarah at every opportunity. And he did speak to her father. William Lord had already suspected that Charles and Sarah were falling in love, and he had given the matter a great deal of thought. He had no objection to Charles as a son-in-law, he explained, but he did not approve of Sarah marrying a sea captain. All too well, he knew of the heartache and worry she would be bound to experience during the long weeks, months, and even years that she waited patiently at home for him to return from his voyages. With no means of communication from ships at sea, she would never know until the day he returned whether he was sick or well, or, perhaps, had been shipwrecked and drowned at some lonely spot on the other side of the world. This, William Lord said, was a way of life that he wanted no daughter of his to have to endure. "Wait a while," he told Charles. Then, after a year or two, if Charles and Sarah still wanted to be married, he would reconsider the matter.

Captain Barry went to Kennebunkport every day. There the *Oakland*'s three tall masts had been stepped, and under the direction of a boss rigger, riggers had set up the spars and yards. For the next three weeks they were busy fitting and placing literally miles of cordage. It required a great deal of work to splice, worm, parcel, and serve all of the complicated rigging and lines that the vessel needed. Sailmakers, with only palms, needles, and other hand tools, fashioned several thousand square feet of hard canvas into properly shaped sails with enough stiffness and "belly" to draw the wind. When she was ready, the *Oakland* had two complete suits of sails, every one of which had had to be tried and fitted.

The fourth of June, the day for the *Oakland* to sail, came all too soon for her captain, who was now more deeply in love than ever with Sarah Lord. Thomas Curtis had come from Boston to see his ship and to purchase locally a partial cargo of lumber to be carried on her first voyage. The *Oakland* would sail to Boston to take on more cargo, then carry her lumber and other goods to Savannah, where they would be exchanged for cotton for Liverpool. A crew for the ship had been recruited, partly from Boston and partly from surrounding towns on the coast of Maine. The first and second mate were Kennebunk men, as it was not until nearly three years later that Thomas Curtis, Junior, joined the *Oakland*.

On sailing day, many people came to Kennebunkport to see the ship. At her head, hanging on each side of her bow, were carved sideboards with the vessel's name on them. These were only for identification in port. They would be unshipped and stowed at all times when the vessel was at sea. The *Oakland* was not a sharp ship, as sailing ships went, but with her square stern, blunt bow, lofty rig, and flush deck, she presented an un-mistakable charm. Sarah called the ship "majestic" when she came aboard briefly to bid Charles good-bye. Both of them would write frequently, they promised each other, as Sarah turned to leave and follow her father down the gangway.

Thomas Curtis took passage aboard the ship to Boston on her maiden voyage, sharing the master's cabin with Captain Barry. He stood on the poop with the captain as the gangway was hauled aboard and the shore lines cast off. As the ship moved slowly away from the wharf, well-wishers shouted fare-wells. The *Oakland*'s master felt certain that he could hear Sarah's voice above all the others. But he could not look shore-ward because all his attention had to be directed to the sailors who were climbing the rigging and beginning to set the sails on the yards. By the time the *Oakland* had reached open water, sails had miraculously appeared on every mast. Not until then could Captain Barry turn and wave to those on the wharf at Kennebunkport. But they were only specks in the distance by this time, and it would be a year or more before he could return to the town and his now "dear Sarah" again.

SARAH CLEAVES LORD (1821-1904)

From a portrait painted by Charles H. Granger in June 1845, the month and year that she married Captain Charles Edward Barry. After her wedding on June twenty-fourth, Sarah chose to call herself Sarah Cleaves Barry rather than use her maiden name, Lord, as her middle name.

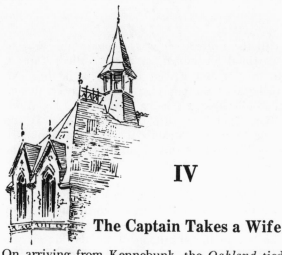

IV

The Captain Takes a Wife

On arriving from Kennebunk, the *Oakland* tied up at Boston's Central Wharf for several days to take on cargo. The ship had handled very well during her maiden voyage from Maine. In every respect, the new vessel lived up to the expectations of both her master and her owner. In due course, Captain Barry sailed for Savannah and thence to Liverpool, loaded to capacity with bales of Georgia cotton, and for the next twelve months, the *Oakland* plied the Atlantic between the United States and Europe. Generally, the ship carried cotton from the southern ports to Liverpool. On her return voyages, she brought manufactured goods from England, which were delivered to Boston, New York, or Philadelphia.

The first of August 1842 found the *Oakland* at Boston, unloading a mixed cargo from Europe. When Thomas Curtis informed Captain Barry that it would be two weeks, or longer, before he was ready to send the ship south after more cotton, the captain decided to take a short vacation and go to Maine. It would be the first time he had seen Sarah since he had left Kennebunk late in June the year before.

Although one could now travel from Boston to Kennebunk and Portland on trains that operated on a more or less regular schedule, there was also at this time a coastal packet steamship service between Boston and Portland that stopped at Kennebunk.

By comparison with the railroad, it was a comfortable way to travel. On the Portland Steamboat, as it was called, Captain Barry left Boston one day and arrived at Kennebunk the next. Now that the Portland to Boston stage line had been discontinued, some of the old stages were being used to meet the trains and steamships. One had been dispatched from The Hilton House to meet the Portland Steamboat at Kennebunkport. Captain Barry availed himself of this opportunity to ride to the inn where, as before, he planned to stay.

Had Charles arrived sooner, he would have been able to help Sarah celebrate her birthday on the seventh of August. As it was, he only missed the event by two days. Fortunately, he remembered the date and brought a belated present when he called at her home late in the afternoon of the day he arrived in town. Sarah, who was both surprised and delighted at this unexpected visit, invited him to stay for supper.

The day had been hot and the evening was delightfully warm. When supper was finished, Sarah suggested that they harness one of her father's horses for a buggy ride to Kennebunk Beach. It would be pleasant, Sarah said, to watch the moon rise when it came up over the ocean. The road, for the most part, was soft sand but it could be easily traveled if the horse were allowed to walk most of the way, she told Charles.

When the couple returned to the house on Summer Street in Kennebunk Village several hours later, Sarah was radiant. Her mother, she found, had gone to bed. Her father was still up. She could hardly wait to tell him that she and Charles were going to be married.

William Lord took the news of his daughter's betrothal quietly. When he finally spoke, he said, " No, Sarah, I won't let you do it. If Charles would leave the sea, I would feel quite differently about it. The way things are, I cannot give you my permission to marry him."

" But, Father," Sarah said, " I no longer need your permission. You forget that I was twenty-one years old, day before yesterday. I am going to marry Charles and there is nothing that you can do to prevent me."

In the end, a compromise was reached. William Lord rather reluctantly gave his consent when it was decided that Charles and Sarah would not be married for quite some time. They would announce their engagement but would not set a wedding date for at least two years. By that time, perhaps, Charles could save enough money to be able to retire from the sea and invest in some business on shore at Kennebunk or Boston. In the interim, he would continue to sail on the *Oakland* and Sarah would stay home to help her mother. But no matter whether Charles could retire by then or not, they would not wait longer than three years before being married.

When his short vacation time was up, Captain Barry returned to Boston and the *Oakland*. During the period that followed while he was literally counting the days until he and Sarah could set the date of their wedding, an interesting incident took place in Boston that is worthy of note from a historical point of view; and as the captain's personal friend and employer Thomas Curtis played a part in this event, it has an indirect connection with the story of Captain Barry's life.

Once the first transatlantic steamship, the *Great Western,* commenced regular service in 1838, she was followed by the British and American Steam Navigation Company's steamer, the *British Queen,* which was put into transatlantic service the following year. The vessel soon became a great rival of the Brunel-built *Great Western.* Transatlantic steamship competition started in earnest when the owners of the *British Queen* added another steamer, the *President,* under the command of Lieutenant Roberts.

Soon, a third transatlantic service, the Cunard Line, was operating steamships between England and the United States. Its founder, Samuel Cunard, had been born in Halifax. When he conceived the idea of opening a transatlantic steamship service, he was the fifty-two-year-old partner of a Boston shipowning firm. His first steamship was the *Britannia,* which he had built on the Clyde in England. The *Britannia* first sailed for Halifax and Boston on July 4, 1840. The second Cunard steamer, the

Caledonia, made her first transatlantic run just a month later. Soon a third vessel, the *Columbia*, was added to the line.

The *President* left New York for England on March 12, 1841, never to be heard from again. The loss of Lieutenant Roberts, his officers, the crew, and a hundred and thirty-six passengers, and the subsequent loss of a mail contract by the owners of the ship brought the collapse of the British and American Steam Navigation Company. This served to intensify the competition between Samuel Cunard and the owners of the *Great Western*. As one line sailed from Boston and the other from New York, it also spawned a great rivalry between the ports as they vied with one another for passenger and freight patronage on the transatlantic steamers.

The Cunard-owned *Britannia* arrived at Boston one bitterly cold day late in January 1843. The next few days were even colder. They were, in fact, the coldest that anyone could remember, and Boston Harbor froze over. The ice effectively closed the port to all shipping. When it was learned that the ice-bound *Britannia* would undoubtedly be prevented from sailing on schedule on the first of February, New York newspapers publicized the situation by proclaiming that Boston was not an all-year port, therefore, New York should be made the American terminus of all transatlantic steamship service, including the Cunard line.

On hearing of this reaction in New York, Mayor Martin Brimmer of Boston appointed a committee of Boston businessmen to determine if it would not be possible to cut the *Britannia* out of the ice. On this committee were Benjamin Rich, Ozias Goodwin, Thomas Smith, Samuel Quincy, Thomas Gray, Charles Brown, Ammi Lombard, and Thomas Curtis. Among themselves, these men subscribed fifteen hundred dollars of their own money, which they used to hire the firm of George Hittinger and Company to cut two canals in the ice. One was from the pier of the East Boston ferry to the open sea, and the other ran from the ferry landing to India Wharf, where the *Britannia* was docked. The canals were promptly and successfully cut. When the *Britannia* left Boston on the third of February, thousands of

spectators went out on the ice to cheer as she made her way through the canals and out to sea. No more was ever said about Boston not being an all-year, all-weather port.

As things worked out for Captain Barry and Sarah Lord, it was not until just before Christmas 1844 that they were able to set a time for their wedding. They would be married, they announced, in June 1845. The date might have been sooner had not Sarah's mother become pregnant again. As soon as it had been known that she would have another child in December, both she and Mr. Lord persuaded Sarah not to be married until after the baby came. She would be needed, they said, to help with the other Lord children until the new baby was at least six months old.

Mary Cleaves Lord was born to Sarah's father and mother at their home on Summer Street in Kennebunk on December 14, 1844. Shortly thereafter, Charles Barry and Sarah disclosed that the date of their wedding would be June 24, 1845, at which time Charles would retire from the sea. He would sail the *Oakland* to England for Thomas Curtis one more time. After that, Thomas Curtis Junior, who had now been first mate for about two years, would replace Captain Barry as master of the vessel.

On February 16, 1845, Captain Barry set sail from Charleston, South Carolina, with a cargo of cotton for Liverpool, on what was to have been his last voyage in the *Oakland*. He anticipated being back in Boston about mid-May, whereupon he would wind up his affairs with Thomas Curtis preparatory to leaving for Kennebunk to be married. Except that he would take a long vacation, part of which would be his honeymoon, his plans for what he would do thereafter remained uncertain.

But the hand of fate often intervenes in the execution of men's best-laid plans. A month and four days after leaving Charleston, the *Oakland* was wrecked during a storm in St. George's Channel, when she was driven on some submerged rocks about half a mile offshore near the hamlet of Rhoscolyn, on the coast of Wales. The second mate and one seaman lost their lives, but Captain Barry and the rest of the crew were

saved. It was not until the first week in June, after the remains of the *Oakland* and her cargo had been salvaged and sold, that the captain could leave England to return to the United States.

Captain Barry boarded the Cunard steamship *Britannia* at Liverpool on the fourth of June for the 2,500-mile Atlantic crossing to Boston via Halifax. The Scots-built ship was 207 feet long and displaced 2,000 tons. Like her sister ships, the *Arcadia, Caledonia,* and *Columbia* (the last named of which had been lost in a fog and wrecked on Cape Sable, Nova Scotia, without loss of life in 1843), the *Britannia* was powered by a 740-horsepower side-lever engine. Her paddle wheels were 28 feet in diameter and turned at 16 revolutions per minute. The vessel was equipped with auxiliary sails, which were used to increase her speed when the wind was favorable. A crew of ninety stoked the fires in her boilers and handled the sails, the mails, and the needs of a hundred and fifteen passengers. A shelter on the deck was provided for cows, which furnished fresh milk every day for the passengers.

Crossing the Atlantic on the *Britannia,* or any other steamship in those days, was no laughing matter. Cramped, unheated staterooms, indifferent food, and the inevitable discomfort of a small crowded ship combined to make the voyage quite unpleasant. When Charles Dickens had crossed the North Atlantic on the *Britannia* in 1843, he had complained bitterly. The ship's saloon, he wrote, was "not unlike a gigantic hearse with windows on the sides." He described his stateroom as an "utterly impracticable, thoroughly hopeless and a profoundly preposterous box." Nevertheless, the transatlantic steamships during the 1840 period offered reliable, safe, and relatively fast transportation at a time when most of the public did not expect luxury.

On Captain Barry's voyage, the *Britannia* arrived at Boston on the sixteenth of June. From Liverpool to Halifax, the ship had nearly equaled the record that had been established by the *Arcadia* in July 1841, when the same passage had been made in nine days and twenty-one hours. In Boston, Captain Barry received confirmation of what he had already been told

by letter, namely, that the insurance underwriters had completely
exonerated him of all blame in the wreck of the *Oakland* and
that Thomas Curtis would be reimbursed by insurance for the
loss of his ship.   In haste, because the time was short, Charles
Barry completed his business in Boston, then took the Portland
packet steamer for Kennebunk.   He arrived on the twenty-second
of June, just two days before the date set for his wedding.

With such a large family, Sarah's mother not feeling well,
and no help around the house except one hired girl, Sarah and
Charles decided upon a small, unpretentious wedding.   Only a
few close friends and relatives were invited to the ceremony,
which was held in the "Governor's Room" of the house on
Summer Street.   Sarah's father was still not very enthusiastic
over his daughter's marrying a sea captain, even though Charles
claimed that he was not going to sea any more.

Sarah and her mother appear never to have been very close.
Indeed, Sarah was on much more intimate terms with her Aunt
Mary Cleaves from nearby Biddeford than she was with her
own mother.   This is understandable because Mrs. Lord was
away from home for nearly half of every year, spending the
winter with her sister in Washington.   Aunt Mary had approved
of Charles Barry from the beginning and had done everything
she could to promote the marriage that would take Sarah away
from the bondage she was under at home.   Reminiscing in
a letter to Sarah later, Charles Barry had this to say about the
wedding:

> Aunt Mary has been so kind to us both that we should both
> endeavor, when in our power, to contribute to her happiness.
> I have often thought how kind it was of her to take the lead
> in our wedding, for she seemed the only one except for the
> two principal actors who felt any interest.   I know that I felt
> a great deal better for having her at Kennebunk and very
> grateful for the interest she felt.   I don't know how you
> would have got through the business without her.

After the wedding, Sarah and Charles were driven by carriage to the new Kennebunk railroad depot at Mitchell's Mill
where they "took the cars" on the Portland, Saco and Ports-

CAPTAIN CHARLES EDWARD BARRY (1811-1851)
From a portrait painted about the time he married Sarah Cleaves Lord, in June 1845.

mouth Railroad to Dover, New Hampshire. Here they left the train to spend the night at an inn before starting a honeymoon trip by stage through the New Hampshire White Mountains. The ride to Dover was the first time that either of them had been on a train. When writing to Sarah about it afterward, Charles commented, " How pleasant it was, you and I sitting cozily upon one seat, making our observations about all we saw."

By 1845 railroad cars had greatly improved over the coaches that had first been used on the early Boston railroads. Rows of forward facing seats on each side of the car, with an aisle between, had replaced the long benches that had been standard in the beginning. But the seats were still anything but comfortable, and the trains still jerked in a most annoying manner. Cars were lighted at night by whale-oil lamps or flickering tallow candles. Ventilation was poor and there were no screens over the windows. Smoke and soot from the engine came in whenever the windows were opened. There were no water coolers in the coaches, though a barrel of water was usually carried in the baggage car. Newsboys carried a bucket of water drawn from this source and a tin cup or dipper for the convenience of the passengers. The maximum number of cars on a train was twelve. Still, so new was all this to Sarah and Charles that they thoroughly enjoyed every minute of their thirty-mile ride from Kennebunk to Dover.

From Dover the newlyweds went by stage to Rochester and thence to Lake Winnepesaukee. They journeyed in a leisurely manner through the White Mountains. At the top of Pinkham Notch, they took an open Concord wagon drawn by four horses that carried them and other sightseers up the steep, narrow road to the top of Mt. Washington. From the summit house (which was replaced in 1853 by the Tip Top House that is still standing today) they could see for over a hundred miles in any direction. Many months afterward, Captain Barry recalled the experience when he wrote:

I recently found a small specimen of the top of Mt. Washington in my desk where it had been placed and forgotten.

It was a piece of rose quartz that was given to a certain young lady by, perhaps, a lover upon the very apex of the mountain. Can you realize, dear Sarah, that it will soon be two years since you and I took a fashionable dinner upon the top of that famous mountain, and how gracefully the guide served out the morsels to us hungry folks?

The honeymoon trip also included a swing through the Green Mountains of Vermont, which went as far as Burlington on the shore of Lake Champlain. From there the couple went to Boston, where they had decided to live. They rented two rooms, consisting of a bedroom and a parlor, on the second floor of a boarding-house owned by a Mrs. Scott at No. 16 Lincoln Street, near the corner of Summer Street.

Captain Barry's feelings about their settling down to married life and housekeeping and the events of the past few months were expressed in a letter he wrote to Sarah later:

I had been roaming all over the world and, at 30 years, was still a bachelor. I was apparently as far from marriage as the farthest, for I had resolved that I would never marry just for the sake of being married. I used to think that I was working for no one but myself, although I often used to wish that I could meet a kindred spirit in the shape of some dear girl with a heart in sympathy with my own. When I went to Kennebunk, little did I dream that I was there to meet one dear being whose heart could bind me closely to its own. Dearest, we were reserved for each other and the event has proved how happy it is for us. Do you not think so, love? Oh, you are a dear, dear girl, and I can never love you too much.

V

To Sea Again

Once Charles Barry and his bride were established in the rooms
they had rented from Mrs. Scott on Lincoln Street, the relatively
young sea captain commenced to look around Boston for something to do. He called on Thomas Curtis and other friends
who were in business in the city, and he spent a great deal of
time at Topliff's News Room, which by then had been moved
to the new Merchants Exchange Building on State Street. He
had saved some money — more than enough to last several years,
yet not a sufficient amount to permit complete retirement at
such an early age. Nor would he have wanted full retirement,
even if he had been able to enjoy such a luxury. Captain
Barry was an active, restless man who needed something to
occupy his mind and time. He could not be happy in idleness.

In an attempt to settle down to a business life on shore,
the captain bought an interest in the steam coastal packet *S. S.
Decatur,* that cruised the Atlantic seaboard. On one occasion,
Captain Barry arranged for the ship to carry a cargo of Maine
granite from Vinalhaven on Vinalhaven Island in Penobscot
Bay to New York. Granite quarrying was a leading industry
in Maine for years. Blocks of Maine granite were much in
demand in the large cities for building construction, while the
smaller pieces were used as paving stones. The product often
made an attractive commodity for the coastal ships to carry. The

Decatur also transported Virginia tobacco from Hampton Roads at Norfolk to Boston and New York, and she carried many other types of cargo. But keeping the *Decatur* on the go and the few other interests he was able to find in Boston were not enough to keep Captain Barry busy. He grew more and more restless with every passing week.

In the fall of 1845, Sarah's father accompanied Mrs. Lord on a trip by steamer from Kennebunk to Washington, where she would again spend the winter with her sister. Aunt Mary Cleaves was left in charge of the Lord children in Maine. On his return to New England late in December, William Lord stopped to visit Charles and Sarah and attend to some business in Boston. He remained for Christmas dinner with the Barrys at Mrs. Scott's. During the course of his visit, Sarah both surprised and pleased her father by announcing that he was to become a grandfather in May. Mr. Lord also learned that except for the financial venture with the *Decatur,* Charles had been unable to find anything to do in Boston that interested him.

After some discussion, it was decided that Charles and Sarah would leave Boston and go to Kennebunk to live. Everything considered, the move made very good sense. Sarah was homesick, Charles had no ties to prevent his leaving the city, and Mr. Lord wanted Sarah under the care of his family doctor in Maine until after her baby came. He pointed out to Charles that business opportunities along the Maine coast were just as numerous as they were in Boston. If anything, it would be easier for Captain Barry to find some enterprise to his liking in a small community than it would be in a large one.

Sarah, Charles, and William Lord went by train to Kennebunk right after New Years, in 1846. The cars they rode on the Eastern Railroad from East Boston to Portsmouth, New Hampshire, were small — scarcely more than thirty-five feet long and eight feet wide. The doors at the ends were narrow and the windows were nailed shut. The cars were stuffy and cold.

When the train on which they were riding stopped out in the country about halfway between Ipswich and Newburyport on the way to Portsmouth, Sarah wanted to know the reason.

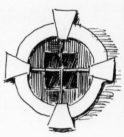

She became even more curious when the train commenced backing up. Her father, who had ridden this same train several times, explained what was happening.

Like most of the other early railroads, the Eastern Railroad was a single-track affair. Side tracks, or turnouts for trains going in the opposite directions to pass one another, were few and far between. It was not until 1851 that Samuel Morse's electric telegraph commenced to be used for train dispatching and for relaying arrival notices when trains came into the various stations. Until that time, there was no method of communication between depots, and trains were seldom on schedule. To solve the problem of their passing each other, a large pole, called a center post, was erected beside the tracks at the halfway point between the turnouts. Whenever a train moving north, such as the one that Sarah and the two men were on, was met by a train moving south before a center post was reached, the northbound train had to stop and back up to the nearest turnout, where it would take to the side track. Had they reached the center post before meeting the southbound train, the train headed south would have had to back up.

The system worked, although more than one head-on collision took place between two trains racing to arrive first at the same center post. At other times, when two trains happened to arrive at a center post almost simultaneously, fist fights between the crews and even the passengers of the two trains occasionally occurred as they tried to settle the question of which train would have to back up. The troubles with turnouts and center posts stemmed from the fact that trains were almost always late. As it was mostly a case of a train being due at a station when it arrived there, the expression " he lies like a timetable " became a figure of speech.

Charles, Sarah, and Sarah's father changed trains at Portsmouth. On arriving at Kennebunk their train was met at Mitchell's Mill by a stagecoach, which carried them to Kennebunk Village.

In a few days, Charles and Sarah Berry rented a suite of two rooms on the second floor of The Hilton House on Tavern Hill.

One was a large east-corner bedroom and the other a small room over the hall on the first floor. The Barrys furnished both rooms with their own furniture.

The record is not clear as to what Captain Barry did between January 1846 and November that same year. Presumably, he endeavored without success to find some gainful occupation in or around Kennebunk. On one occasion, he and Sarah went to Portland, twenty-five miles northeast of Kennebunk. Although the Portland to Boston stage line had been discontinued when rail service between the two cities became available, stages still operated locally among the towns of the Maine coast. Captain Barry noted the trip by stage back from Portland to Kennebunk in a letter he wrote to Sarah in 1849:

> It is three years ago today since we were traveling from Portland in the stage with the noted John Smith, with his single eye, as the driver. I well remember when we stopped for dinner at Saco. The landlord sorted his guests and charged me 50 cents for each of our dinners because I was " city folks." He only charged the other passengers twenty-five cents because they were not " city folks." We had a good laugh about it.

Sarah's baby was born in the Barry suite at Hilton's on May 15, 1846. The child was a boy whom Charles and Sarah named William Edward. Their nickname for him was " Little Willie." Both mother and son did very well and soon Sarah was up and about again, feeling as fit as ever.

Although the summer passed quickly, Captain Barry became increasingly discontented because he could not find anything to do with himself. Many times he considered returning to sea but dared not mention the subject to Sarah or his father-in-law. Finally, during October, Captain Barry received a letter from a man named William F. Parrott in Boston. Parrott, it seemed, was a former sea captain from Portsmouth, New Hampshire, who had retired to become a merchant-ship owner, operating out of Boston. One of his ships, the *Delhi,* lay idle in Boston Harbor because Parrott could not find a competent master to take command of her. In some desperation, he had turned to

his friend Thomas Curtis for help. Curtis had suggested that he try to persuade Captain Barry in Kennebunk to recruit a crew and take the ship to sea. Would Charles Barry, Parrott asked in his letter, be kind enough to come to Boston and talk the matter over?

To the captain's surprise, neither Sarah nor her father expressed opposition when he showed them Parrott's letter. They both realized by now that he had been a sailor for too many years to be able to be happy with any other life until, at least, he was somewhat older than he was in 1846. Secretly, perhaps, William Lord even welcomed the opportunity to have Sarah at home once more during the long intervals when Charles would be gone. And no one could deny that Sarah's mother certainly needed her help running the big house and caring for the family on Summer Street.

Charles Barry " took the cars " to Boston to talk with Captain Parrott. When he returned, he announced that he had agreed to sail for Parrott as master of the *Delhi*. The vessel was a three-masted, square-rigged sailing ship of 608 tons that had been built at Medford, Massachusetts, in 1838. She was 140 feet long, had a beam of 30 feet and a draft of 15 feet. The ship had two decks, a square stern and a billethead, and like the other freighters of her day, was painted black with a white waist dotted with black ports that opened into the between-decks space. Parrott had a contract with Frederick Tudor to carry ice from Boston to Bombay and Calcutta. The hull of the *Delhi* had therefore been double sheathed to prevent the ice from melting. If a crew for the ship could be recruited in time, Captain Parrott had told Captain Barry that he wanted the vessel to sail for India as near to the first of December as possible. The round-trip voyage would last a year.

By 1846 Tudor's ice export business had more than doubled what it had been eight years earlier when Captain Barry carried a cargo of ice to Charleston in the bark *Madagascar*. Tudor was now loading from both Gray's Wharf at Charlestown and India Wharf in Boston, and he kept enough ice in storage from winter to winter to be able to ship it all the year round. There was hardly a warm country in the world on which vessels carrying ice for Frederick Tudor did not call. Indeed, Tudor ice from one particular source — Wenham Lake at Wenham, Massachusetts — had earned such a reputation for its purity and hardness that it commanded premium prices, particularly in England, whenever it could be obtained.

The Barrys gave up their suite at the Hilton House about the middle of November. Sarah and "Little Willie" moved to her father's home on Summer Street and Charles left shortly thereafter for Boston. With him he took a Kennebunk man named Barnes, whom he had hired to be the *Delhi*'s first mate.

It had been with a very heavy heart that Charles had bid farewell to his wife of seventeen months and to his adored young son. The parting had been a sad one, particularly for Sarah. A few days later, Charles wrote to her from his room at the United States Hotel in Boston. "I hope, dearest, you have been able to drive off the unpleasant feeling which surrounded you when I left," he said. "I know and feel, my love, the un-

pleasant feelings experienced by hearts that love when the hour of separation arrives. But we must try to overcome them, as we must every other trial which we know has to be met."

December 1, 1846, found the *Delhi* tied up at Gray's Wharf, loading ice. Tudor was now using specially built, insulated freight cars for transporting ice from his many lakeside storage warehouses directly to the point of loading. Big blocks of ice were taken directly from the railroad cars to the gigs that ran up and down on the tracks of the ship-loading apparatus. Improved methods of handling the ice had increased the rate of loading a vessel to five hundred tons a day instead of three hundred. When the last ice had gone down the chutes into the hold of the *Delhi* and the ice had been covered with sawdust, two hundred barrels of the best Baldwin apples were securely stowed on top of the ice. Then the hatches were battened down and sealed.

On Sunday, December 6, Captain Barry again wrote to Sarah:

Our day for sailing is fixed for Tuesday and we shall go without doubt if the wind is right. I intend tomorrow night to mail a letter for you and will enclose in it about $140 which I hope may reach you safe. Do you think that will be enough? If not, you may go on tick for another $100 [i.e., borrow that amount]. And while I am now writing and have time, I will take the opportunity, dearest Sarah, of expressing to you how happy I have been in your society, and in my choice of a life companion. You have been to me all that a good wife could be. Your thoughtful affections have always clung closely around me. You have ever been interested and anxious for my welfare. You have made my home always happy to me. I confess to you that I have been perfectly satisfied, without one fault to find or one complaint to make. I think it is unnecessary for me to here express how truly devotedly and fondly I love you. Yes, yes, dearest you are the dearest earthly object to me.

Unfavorable weather prevented the *Delhi* from sailing on Tuesday Wednesday, December 9, found Captain Barry writing another letter to Sarah:

Here I am, once more in Boston, awaiting to get my good ship *Delhi* to sea. The wind hangs to the north, accompanied by rain and snow. I do not like the opportunity that offers today very well for going to sea and shall most likely hold where I am. I'm not anxious to get to sea unless the weather looks promising. You need feel no anxiety on that account as I should not be very fond of putting to sea in this wintry season unless the wind and weather looked such as promised to run me well off the coast. The sun was out at noon but the man in the telegraph office [i.e., the office of the Semaphore Telegraph Company on Central Wharf] tells me that there is an easterly wind in the bay. Therefore, instead of going to sea, I shall write this letter to my dear Sarah, and then some others, and trust to tomorrow's luck.

On Thursday, the tenth, Captain Barry rose early, packed his carpetbag, and checked out of the United States Hotel. Upon arriving at Gray's Wharf at Charlestown, he found that Mr. Barnes, the first mate he had hired at Kennebunk, had the ship ready to sail. The *Delhi*'s clearance papers had been made out and the ship's stores for the long voyage that lay ahead had been taken aboard. Over a dozen pigs were grunting in a sty on the deck. Near them were a number of hatches that contained an assortment of poultry — seven dozen hens, one dozen geese, and two dozen ducks. There was also a pen full of sheep and below, between-decks, were sizable stores of the less perishable vegetables — carrots, turnips, winter squash, and pumpkins. The harbor pilot who would guide the *Delhi* down Boston Harbor to Boston Light was already there. As Captain Barry greeted him and the two men shook hands, the last of the *Delhi*'s crew came up the gangway, carrying their duffel bags over their shoulders.

About 9:00 A.M., a Concord wagon with three seats, drawn by a prancing team of chestnut horses drove up on the wharf. The vehicle stopped near the gangway and a Mr. Daniels, who had taken passage to Bombay on the ship, stepped out. He was followed by several friends who had come to see him off. Two sailors came from the *Delhi* to carry Mr. Daniels' trunk to the small stateroom he would occupy, next to the master's cabin. The party boarded the ship where they were met by Captain Barry.

A few minutes later, a carriage arrived bearing Captain Parrott and his chief clerk, as well as Thomas Curtis, who had come to bid farewell to Charles Barry. Then, yet another vehicle drove up on the wharf. Two men got out and boarded the ship, carrying a heavy, well-filled duffel bag between them. Who they were and why they were there is best described by Captain Barry in a letter he wrote to Sarah that night:

Our passenger, Mr. Daniels, came on board with some friends. And then another gent came — a Mr. Whitcomb who has, for years, tended the office at the Tremont House. He brought his young brother who has taken it into his head that he must go to sea. Mr. Whitcomb has educated the boy and brought him up. He has got him a job with me as an apprentice boy in hopes that he will become both sea sick and sick of the sea. He has fitted the boy out in a sailor's rig and he came to see him off. The poor fellow little knows the discomforts he will meet in his undertaking of a sea life. I think that I can judge for him, as I once made such a beginning. I have not forgotten to this day my feelings at that time. But I think of them now only to laugh at them. . . . .

The weather is beautiful and pleasant, and the prospects are good that our good ship will get to sea today. Everything is ready. When I ran down the hotel steps this morning and got in my carriage, I thought of you. Soon after I got to the ship, the last of the sailors and their baggage came bundling aboard. The pilot was there and we began to make active preparations to start. But no wind, no wind! The pilot suggests that we take a steamboat and tow the ship down the harbor. There may be a wind there from the southwest. Captain Parrott feels anxious to have the ship out of his sight and I feel anxious to have her away from Charlestown. I am tired of trailing over to Charlestown two or three times a day. I have engaged the tow boat *R. B. Forbes* to come and take the ship to sea.

At twelve-thirty, the tow boat arrived and drew alongside the *Delhi*. A heavy line from the stern of the *R. B. Forbes* was

made fast to the *Delhi*'s bow. Mr. Daniels' friends and all the rest who were not going to sail left the ship, and the gangway was hauled aboard. Shore lines to the wharf were cast off. The harbor pilot and Captain Barry stood together beside the helmsman on the poop. The towboat blew her whistle as the towline tightened. The *Delhi* eased away from the wharf and into the deep water at the mouth of the Charles River.

That evening by the light of a candle at his desk in his cabin, Captain Barry finished his letter to Sarah:

About one o'clock, we cast-off from the wharf. Tom Curtis gave me a shake of the hand before he left the ship. On the wharf, Captain Parrott and his chief clerk sang out, " Good Bye, Captain Barry," and off we went. I thought of you, love, all the way down the harbor, and scarcely anyone else. The further we proceeded, the more unfavorable the weather looked, promising an easterly wind and snow. I told the pilot to anchor the ship at Nantasket Roads, which he did about 3:00 P.M. The steam boat cast off, gave a toot, and went back to Boston. The weather was cold and miserable.

Evening came, and with it, an easterly wind and thick snow. Then I sat down to finish this letter to my dear Sarah. I am leaving home under new aspects for me. New ties have been formed which bind me by stronger chains of affection than ever before. I am on the point of absenting myself for a year from my dear wife and child. It would be strange if my feelings were not quite as buoyant as usual. I am afraid that my dear Sarah will think I have sailed and feel anxious for me, and, perhaps, pass a sleepless night. I wish that I could tell her that we were comfortably at anchor. But I can only invoke the blessings of Him who has power over all upon her and our dear boy.

Friday, December 11th — The wind this morning was at the northwest and blowing very strong. It was snowing very thick. We could only remain at anchor. After dinner at noon, I made a signal to the pilot for us to start, then came down to finish this letter to Sarah to send by him when he leaves. Even now, it is still very thick and smoky over Boston. Only a few steeples and the Bunker Hill Monu-

ment raise their heads to be seen. We are underway and about four o'clock, the pilot will leave when we pass the lighthouse and bid adieu to our native city.

About one-thirty in the afternoon, Mr. Barnes sent men aloft in the rigging to trim the main and mizzenmasts for the first tack, and he had them brace the yards for the second tack. "Heave short!" was his next command. Men on the forecastle head then commenced working a hand-operated capstan to haul in all the slack in the anchor cable. It was slow, laborious work. Getting the ship under way was a tricky business. The *Delhi* had to be under control by the time the anchor was off the bottom. But if Mr. Barnes set his sails while the anchor was still down, then the ship would struggle about in all directions and the windage of her sails would make it almost impossible to dislodge the anchor from the bottom. If he did not have the sails set and the ship under proper control when the anchor came free, then the ship would commence to drift helplessly.

So Mr. Barnes first "hove short" to bring in enough of the anchor cable so there would be only a few more fathoms still to be taken in before the anchor came off the bottom. Next, all sails were loosened and the sailors prepared to overhaul the running gear while the sails were being set. "Set the tops'ls," was the next order by Mr. Barnes. The six topsails — two on each mast — were set as quickly as possible.

All hands were put to work. The ship's carpenter and the sailmaker were sent to the forecastle head to handle the jib sheets, and a couple of men were on the poop to handle the spanker. The cook handled the foresheet because it was close to his galley. Then the anchor capstan was manned again and more cable was pulled in. When the anchor cable hung straight up and down, indicating that the cable still out was equal to the depth of the water, Mr. Barnes shouted, "Up and down!" Then he commanded, "Break her out!" and up came the anchor. Immediately, the *Delhi* commenced to move. The ship pivoted, at first, then her backed foreyards canted her head around until

the ship was headed in the right direction. All sails were set
as quickly as possible.

It was just a little after 4:00 P.M. when Mr. Barnes slowed
the ship down to meet the small boat that had been sent out
from Boston Light to pick up the pilot. Captain Barry and the
pilot shook hands. The pilot climbed over the rail and went
down the ship's ladder, taking with him the letter that Captain
Barry had written to Sarah, and a letter Mr. Daniels, the passenger, had written. The *Delhi* was on her way to India.

When Captain Barry had engaged the towboat *R. B. Forbes*
on a day without wind to take the *Delhi* through the channels
of Boston Harbor to Nantasket Roads off George's Island, he
had, in small measure, participated in an important epic of
American maritime history. The *R. B. Forbes* was the first
steam towboat to be built specifically for this purpose in the
world. It was also one of the first successful American vessels
to be propelled by screw propellers instead of paddle wheels.
The Archimedean screw is more than two thousand years old,
yet it was not until 1836 that this principle was used to propel
a sizable ship. In 1839, the sea-going steamer *Archimedes* showed
her real worth when she accomplished runs at ten miles an hour
in England. Isambard Kingdom Brunel's 322-foot steamship
Great Britain was the first large propeller-driven ship to cross
the Atlantic, which she did in 1845 — the same year that the
R. B. Forbes was built.

The *R. B. Forbes* was named for her owner, Robert Bennett
Forbes of Boston. Born in 1805, Forbes had the most original
brain and the most attractive personality of any New England
shipowner of his generation. Shipping before the mast at the
age of thirteen, he rose to master at twenty-one and commanded
a ship that he himself owned at twenty-eight. He sailed primarily to China and the Orient and was known as one of the best
authorities on the China trade. He retired from sailing in 1840
to become a merchant-shipper in Boston, where he engaged in
many picturesque and benevolent activities.

An early convert to the screw propeller and iron ships,
Forbes would have had Massachusetts take the lead in steam as

she had in sail. He introduced auxiliary steamers in Chinese waters and he hired the young, twenty-one-year-old marine architect, Samuel Harte Pook of Boston, to design the 300-ton iron towboat, the *R. B. Forbes*. This twin-screw, two-engine steamship was built for Forbes by Otis Tufts at East Boston in 1845. It proved immediately successful and useful in rendering assistance to vessels in distress, in towing big ships at sea, and in getting sailing craft in and out of port. But because of the expense involved, sailing ships rarely used the towboat except when wind and weather conditions made it a necessity.

Aboard the *Delhi*, Captain Barry and the crew settled down to their duties. Not long after the pilot was dropped at Boston Light and the ship commenced to make sail, the captain took two bearings on points on shore. From these, he plotted the ship's position on the chart in the charthouse. He set this down in the ship's official log as the time and position of the *Delhi's* departure. That night he wrote in his own personal journal: " The wind freshened and by eight o'clock brought us down to double reefed topsails. At nine o'clock, we passed the light on Cape Cod, which is the last we shall see of our native land until we return."

Up until the time that the *Delhi* had dropped the pilot, all the ship's crew had worked together to accomplish all that had to be done to get the ship to sea. Just before dark, Mr. Barnes and the second mate — a man from Boston — had stood on the deck near the poop to select their respective watches from the men who made up the crew. In somewhat the manner of men choosing sides before a baseball game, Mr. Barnes and the second mate had alternately selected a man by name from the crew, who had gathered at the ship's waist. Each man, as his name was called, had stepped forward and gone to either the port or starboard rail, depending upon which watch he was going to be on. There he joined the men with whom he would work, eat, and sleep throughout the voyage.

During the division of the crew, Captain Barry had been busy in the charthouse, laying out the *Delhi's* course. When

Mr. Barnes informed him that the port and starboard watches had been formed, the captain stepped briefly to the poop from where he addressed the men who had gathered together on the deck. It was a simple, straightforward talk in which the captain made it quite plain to his crew that he expected every one of them to obey orders and do their duty as proper seamen should. He told them that they would find him easy to get along with if they pulled together and did their work well when on duty. But if any man shirked his duty or became insubordinate, then things would go hard with him.

From now on, Mr. Barnes would always be the direct representative of Captain Barry in every detail pertaining to handling the ship. The captain, like all autocrats in other walks of life, had but few pleasures beyond the display of his dignity and the occasional exercise of his supreme authority during the entire time he was afloat. He was never on intimate terms with anyone aboard the vessel. Captain Barry himself wrote, " The captain is the most idle man in the ship. Time hangs heavily upon his hands. But, then, he has more time to think, and you may rest assured that his thoughts are mostly on some dear ones, far away."

The second mate's berth was anything but a pleasant one, for he was neither an officer nor a seaman. Like the first officer, Mr. Barnes, the second mate was responsible while on duty for the proper conduct of the ship's work. But unlike Mr. Barnes, he actually had to work with the men of his watch when they engaged in any phase of seamanship, such as going aloft to reef or furl sails, and even in the more disagreeable tasks such as oiling and greasing the ship's gear and tarring down the decks. The second mate was expected to enforce orders and maintain his dignity, but on account of his close association with the men, they were apt to have little regard for him as an officer. His quarters were aft with Captain Barry's and Mr. Barnes's cabins, and he took his meals at the same table as they did, but never with them. The captain and the first mate usually had their meals together, the second mate taking what was left.

In addition to the two mates and three apprentice boys, the rest of the *Delhi*'s crew consisted of sixteen men who, in Captain Barry's words, were "gathered from all quarters of the world, and no doubt, could speak as many languages as were spoken at the Confusion of Tongues at the building of the Tower of Babel." Many were in their late teens or early twenties. The older men among them were, for the most part, victims of drink who squandered their wages at the end of each voyage in traditional sailor fashion. After a spree ashore, they had no other recourse except to re-ship. The majority of the men wore a distinctive costume: Shiny black tarpaulin hat, red checked shirt, blue bell-bottomed dungaree trousers and a navy-blue pea jacket.

Captain Barry's regard for the average sailor was not very high. Writing in his personal journal, he had this to say about them:

> To take sailors generally, as a class, they are, in my opinion of them, miserable drunks. It is true that there are some exceptions among them but, as a body, the more I know of them, the less sympathy I have for them. When they are on board my ship, under my charge, I will, of course, do everything for them which a sense of right and duty calls for on my part. But there is very little that I would put myself out of the way to do for a sailor at large who is not employed by me. To be brought in contact and have to do with sailors is one of the most disagreeable parts of a seafaring life. And 99 out of every 100 masters and officers, if you should ask them, will say the same thing.

Speaking specifically of the crew of the *Delhi* on the voyage to Bombay, Captain Barry conceded that "as a whole, they are a very civil and well behaved crew."

The first mate, Mr. Barnes, was a rather attractive widower of medium build who had a light, ruddy complexion, sandy hair, and whiskers. His age was about thirty-five. He had been at sea for many years on both merchant ships and men-of-war. He read a great deal and was a pleasant, intelligent conversationalist. When running the ship, he was a clear-headed officer who could make the right decision and make it quickly in an emergency. He was a reliable, experienced, and very capable seaman.

The second mate was a man named Cabot who had been born near Boston, at Lexington. He was older than Captain Barry and Mr. Barnes and a confirmed bachelor. Captain Barry described him as " one of those still, quiet bodies that never says anything. He appears to be quite domestic in his habits, but a thorough old bachelor in all his ways. I set him down as past all hope. He is a man of good disposition."

The *Delhi*'s apprentice boys consisted of Adam Whitcomb, whose older brother worked at the Tremont House in Boston (" He's a good little fellow," wrote Captain Barry in his journal), and two other boys, both named Charles. The father of one was a former ship's master who operated a ship chandlery on Commercial Street in Boston. The other was the son of a Unitarian minister at Troy, New York.

The ship's carpenter was a Swede, of whom Captain Barry said, " I know nothing of him other than that he is a steady fellow and a first-rate carpenter." His duties and those of the sailmaker kept these two men employed during the daylight hours. Together with the steward and cook, they were excused from standing watch with the other members of the crew. Unless it was a matter of " all hands on deck," these men were able to obtain an undisturbed sleep at night. The ship's steward had charge of the pantry. He provided the provisions to the cook from which the meals for the officers and the crew were prepared. He waited on the captain personally, and while actually a member of the crew, was seldom considered as one of them. The cook occupied a position somewhat nearer to the crew. It meant something to be on friendly terms with him, partly because his warm galley was a fine place to dry socks or light a pipe on a sloppy night.

Captain Barry colorfully described the *Delhi*'s steward and cook in his personal journal:

My steward is one of the distinguished great. His name is Cooper. His grandmother was a white woman and his mother black. His father was an Indian and a coachman to old General Cooper of Delaware for 28 years. His mother had 25 children of whom my distinguished steward is one of six twins who were born at three different births. He had the honor to be born into the world feet first which, I suppose, in some way accounts for his feet being so large. He has been married, but while absent at sea, he left an order for his wife to receive half his monthly wages. On his return from a voyage, he found that his dear one had found some other gentleman of distinction and was living with him, apparently having forgotten that she had a husband at sea. But it seems that she did not forget to get the money from the half-pay order.

The cook was born near James River, in Virginia. He is about as black as the blackest. His complexion is so dark that, beside him, ebony is brilliant white. His history, to me, is somewhat obscure as I have never taken the trouble to inquire about it. The other day, he came aft to draw some molasses from a barrel which stands on deck. I told him I was very glad to learn two things about him — that he was learning to spell and that he had a sweetheart. I told him that I should keep an eye on him in port to see that he did not forget her. He says there is no danger of that sin.

By the end of the first ten days at sea, the *Delhi* was encountering much better and a great deal warmer weather. At dusk on the twenty-second of December — the shortest day of the year — Captain Barry left his cabin to walk the deck for exercise. Ahead, the sea turned white as the bow of the ship plowed through the water. Aloft, three pyramids of sails billowed gracefully on the ship's tall masts. The wind sang in the taut rigging. Aft on the poop, a young seaman stood at the wheel, steering competently, with just a touch of the spokes. The captain thought to himself that a full-rigged sailing ship was not only the loveliest thing in the world but also the most nearly perfect of man's sea-borne creations. That night he wrote in his journal:

Oh, it is such a delightful evening. The sea is smooth and calm; the weather mild and pleasant, while the new moon

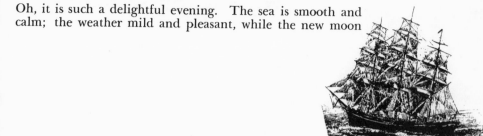

sheds a bright luster in company with myriads of stars all
around. The sky is a beautiful blue without one single speck
of cloud to mar the beauty of it all.

VI

Four Months to Bombay

Not long after sailing from Boston, Captain Barry decided to change the style of his personal journal. It had been his original intent to keep an informal record of the voyage to Bombay by setting his thoughts down on paper every few days. But every time he wrote in the journal, this lonesome, homesick man found himself unconsciously writing a letter to his beloved Sarah. "As I am keeping my journal only for her," he wrote, "I shall henceforth address myself to her directly. My journal shall be an epistolary."

The voyage to India is best told in Captain Barry's own words. His journal, in effect, becomes a continuous letter to Sarah, which took over four months to write. On arriving at Bombay, the captain mailed his "epistolary," as he called it, to Sarah at Kennebunk. Then he wrote a similar account of his voyage home, commencing when he set sail, Boston bound, from Calcutta. A large part of both of these journals is trivial chitchat about people and situations back home, and much is repetitious. In Captain Barry's personal account of the Boston to Bombay voyage, which follows, only those parts of his journal are quoted that pertain specifically to the voyage or to him and Sarah. At the end of each entry, he carefully recorded the latitude and longitude of the *Delhi* for that particular date so that the progress of the voyage might be readily followed.

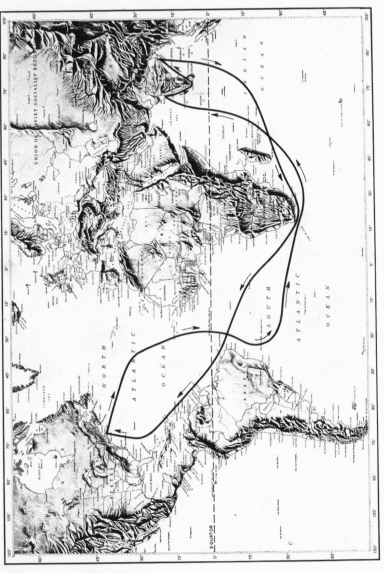

THE INDIA VOYAGES OF CAPTAIN BARRY

Between 1846 and 1849, Captain Barry sailed the ship *Delhi* from Boston to Bombay and Calcutta and return on two different occasions. His outward bound and homeward bound courses were almost identical on both voyages. Each leg of these trips was about 15,000 miles long and required four months of sailing. As can be seen here, the course he followed from Boston to India was quite different from that between India and Boston, because the ocean currents and the direction of the prevailing winds were different.

After departing from Boston, the *Delhi*'s course carried the ship in a southeasterly direction until the mid-Atlantic was reached, about halfway between Cape Hatteras, North Carolina, and the Canary Islands, off the coast of Africa. The ship then turned south to take advantage of the trade winds. The course even veered a little west to parallel the Brazilian coast from Natal to a point off Rio de Janeiro; then southeasterly again to round the Cape of Good Hope close to the African coast between Capetown and Port Elizabeth. Thence the ship made a long, sweeping turn to pass to the east of the Island of Madagascar and on north to Bombay on the northwestern coast of India. The equator was crossed twice and the total distance covered was in excess of fifteen thousand miles.

This is the story that Captain Barry told:

Friday, December 25 — A warm and pleasant day has ushered in Merry Christmas 1846. We passed around the usual compliments of the season. The steward graced his dinner table with all the little luxuries he could muster by way of keeping the day. The sailors came in for a little extra fun for themselves.

December 27 — Sixteen days since leaving the pilot and our third Sunday at sea. The weather is delightful and pleasant and everything is going well. I can imagine that my dear Sarah has just consigned little Willie to someone's care and trotted herself off to church, no doubt glad to breathe the fresh air and feel its invigorating effects.

Not the least of Captain Barry's troubles on the outbound voyage were destined to center around his passenger, Mr. Daniels, who, the captain soon discovered, was suffering from tuberculosis. The journal entry for December 27 continues in this manner:

Mr. Daniels is rather on the sick list and has looked and appeared quite unwell for some days past. He says this voyage is an experiment with him and may operate for or against his complaints. For my part, I think a physician does wrong to recommend to a patient whose lungs are

affected that he go to sea. I think the possibility of the voyage improving his lungs is a very faint one. Everyone knows that the humid and heavy air upon the ocean is directly opposed to assisting sickly lungs. And then, a ship is such an uncomfortable place for a person unaccustomed to the sea. It seems strange that a physician will recommend a patient to take a long voyage — a year — when, if it should prove unfavorable to the disease, the disease has time to become seated, arrive at maturity and have a fatal termination. How much better to send them to a warm climate, to a place of suitable elevation.

December 31 — I thought that I would write in my journal yesterday, but the wind was fresh and a cross sea was running. Writing at sea is not very comfortable unless the sea is smooth. I wonder if you can imagine me seated in my cabin, my desk upon a little shelf but rather too low to write comfortably. To make it better, I have laid an India rubber cushion upon the desk and the Morse's Atlas on top of that, which gives an even, smooth surface for the paper to lay upon. This is the last day of December — the dying day of 1846. Soon, another New Year will break upon us, and leaving the last to be recorded among the things that are past and gone, never more to be brought again before us. How many thoughts and associations are brought into mind at this annual period. And when I look back upon the past year and realize how happy it has been to me, and how much I have enjoyed the society of those friends I dearly love, I would lift up my heart in thankful praise to the Giver of all this good, and ask that these blessings may long be continued to me and mine. How many who commenced the past year with us in the full bloom of life and hope have had it taken away. How many who commenced the year in health, prosperity and happiness have had all their worldly prospects overthrown, their health and happiness blasted, while I, with all my dear friends, have been permitted to continue with no changes but those which added to our happiness.

January 1, 1847 — How many of the few past New Year's days have I been either in port or so situated that I could sit down and write a letter to my dear Sarah, and it has always afforded me great pleasure to do so. But now I'm on the wide, wide sea and can only make up for that privation by writing a few lines in my journal.

A month has passed since I was separated from my own dearest Sarah for a year's long absence. Yes, love, it is just over four weeks since my lips were pressed to thine own sweet lips, and my cheeks were dampened with thy tears of anguish, thy bosom was pressed to mine, and our hearts beat with responsive sadness. It seems a great while to me, dearest Sarah, since I left home and I often picture you to myself. Little Willie sitting in the high chair at the table, looking up and laughing while the other children at home play and talk with him. How glad I shall be to again meet you all after I have been absent a year. I don't know that I have ever felt more contented and easy at sea than I do now. I have much to be grateful for to that great and good Parent who watches over us and bestows upon me so much happiness.

In another few months, it will have been five years since we have known and loved each other — and how immensely loved. Time has already told and proved that we and we alone were the most proper judges of the suitability of our attachment. We have the satisfaction of knowing that we have happily loved and lived. No one can be so dear to me as you are, my dear Sarah, and I trust that I hold as permanent a place in your affections. I will close my January 1st writing by sending you all my love and kisses with the wish of a happy, happy New Year.

Sunday, January 10 — Today the weather is moderately warm and pleasant. I am sitting at my desk dressed in thin clothes, without stock, vest or jacket. The thermometer registers 80° while with you, I expect, you have to make yourself comfortable before a grate glowing with bright coals.

On nineteenth-century sailing ships, the captain served as the ship's doctor. Medicine chests were a standard part of a ship's equipment. Hardly more than a few days ever went by that Captain Barry did not have at least one patient under his care:

January 12 — I have one patient with fever and ague and have taken the preliminary steps for his cure. That is, scouring him out with tartar emetic and a cathartic, preparatory to prescribing quinine. I expect in a few days to have him well.

Mr. Daniels has not been at all well. His constitution is very weak. The slightest change or draft of air makes its impression on him. He does not seem to meet with the improvement in his health that he anticipated. His cough and frequent night sweats trouble him. I think he has a disease of the liver as well as consumption.

January 15 — This is my 36th birthday and you, dearest Sarah, will be 26 in August. How time does fly. As our good Aunt Mary says, " Nothing can beat it but the cars." Often and often do I think of you, dearest. You are the source of my happiness and how readily could I sacrifice all for you. I have always loved you so much. You have been such a kind and good wife to me that it has always been my pride and happiness to do that which I thought would best promote yours. Have I not proved to you that you are the dearest object of my heart?

My patient with fever and ague has become convalescent.

In the days before ships carried wireless and radio, the whereabouts of a ship at sea was never known until the vessel reached port. Weeks and even months passed before a ship's owner and the families or friends of the crew knew whether or not the passage had been a safe one. When ships passed each other at sea, they tried to "speak" to each other. That is, pass close enough so they could communicate by shouting or signaling back and forth. Having identified another vessel at sea, a captain on reaching port would report the time and place at which he had seen the other ship. This information was forwarded by the fastest available means to the vessel's home port for the benefit of her owners and others. The newspapers carried this information. In the *Portland* (Maine) *Transcript,* for instance, under the heading MARINE JOURNAL, ships' names and other pertinent data appeared daily under the sub-

headings " Arrivals," " Spoken " and, lastly, in a black-lined box, " Disasters." One can readily imagine how anxiously Sarah Barry, sitting at home at Kennebunk, hastily opened every issue of the *Portland Transcript* when it arrived and quickly turned to the Marine Journal. Being aware of this, Captain Barry always endeavored to be seen and spoken by other ships at sea whenever he could:

January 24 — I have been in hopes all along that we should pass near enough to some other vessel to get reported but I doubt if we shall now. Last night, a ship passed about a mile to the windward of us. Had it been in daylight, we should have probably been engaged in signals with him. I would like to speak another ship and be reported as I know it would be some satisfaction to you to read that we have been spoken. But now we are almost out of the track of homeward bound vessels and you will probably have to wait to get the first report of us from Bombay.

Do you know, my love, that I have hardly dared to read again any of the letters that you sent me in Boston. I have not been out long enough, and I must not begin to read any of them over until I get eastward of the Cape of Good Hope. Then I shall be about half-passage. If I read them again now, I might feel a little dull and think too much of home. On the homeward passage, I shall allow myself to think of home with perfect liberty and without restraint because every day will bring me nearer to it. But outward bound, it's just the reverse and every day carries me farther from all the dear ones left behind.

February 1 — Save for Mr. Daniels, we are all well except Mr. Barnes, the mate, who has taken a violent cold. I gave him an emetic, soaked his feet and put roasted onions on his chest.

February 7 — Mr. Barnes has not yet gone on duty and, as a consequence, I have stood his watches. I could have deputized someone to keep them but thought I should be faithful in looking after the ship, and have kept the watches myself.

One might imagine that once the *Delhi* was at sea and everything had been put in "sea order," there would not have been much for Captain Barry to do or supervise when he stood the first mate's watches for him. But this was not the case. The inevitable rule aboard the old square-riggers was that every man "on watch" should be kept busy on some kind of work except during the night and on Sundays. Idleness was never tolerated. As soon as there was light enough to see, the morning watch was put to scrubbing and swabbing the decks, coiling loose rigging, polishing the ship's bell and the brass on the binnacle, and doing other odd jobs that the mate in charge of the watch might think up for them. Much of the work was in the nature of repairs to the sailing gear. The standing rigging was regularly examined, tightened, strengthened, and replaced. This meant continual work on the shrouds, stays, preventer-stays, and backstays. And every Saturday, the carpenter oiled and greased all the working parts of the masts, the blocks, and the steering gear. It was a prodigious job.

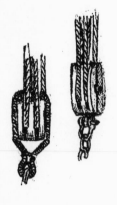

For the daytime watches, the running rigging always demanded close attention, and the halyards, lifts, and braces were always needing repair. Chafing-gear had to be taken off, mended, and put back wherever the countless yards of lines came into contact with the standing rigging. Making rope yarn from pieces of old rope, which sailors would "unlay," knot together, and roll into balls, frequently provided almost constant employment for several sailors. Often, two or three men would be kept busy for days operating a crude device set up on deck to twist rope yarn into spun yarn, which was used to make chafing-gear, for serving ropes, bending sails, and many other purposes. Picking oakum was another duty that the mate in charge of a watch often fell back upon to keep his men busy, especially during sloppy weather. With the sewing of sails under the supervision of the sailmaker, and the painting, varnishing, polishing, scraping, rubbing, greasing, and oiling of every conceivable object aboard the ship, the crew of the *Delhi* were never at a loss for something to do. They also had to take turns doing a two-hour "trick" at the wheel as well as hauling and pulling on the

halyards, sheets, and braces when setting, reefing, and furling the sails in connection with working the ship.

February 15 — Mr. Barnes has returned to duty and today I have been thinking about a letter from my dear, dear wife that will probably be paddling its way down Boston Harbor in one of the Cunard steamers on its way to England. From there, it will go in another steamer to Bombay and be ready to greet me upon my arrival on the shores of India. It will contain news of more than two months later date than I had when I left Boston. I assure you, dear Sarah, I shall feel anxious enough to get hold of it and glean its contents — to know how you all do and how our little boy gets on. I expect bravely, for I can imagine him quite a stout lad by this time with a full-tuned voice that makes itself heard when his wants are not supplied or his will not gratified. How often I think of the little fellow, and how glad I shall be to see him. I shall walk the deck this evening and think of my letter which starts from Boston today. I often think, dear Sarah, how long it will seem for you to wait for a letter from me, for you cannot receive one before the middle of next July.

Sunday, March 7 — What a long time it has been since I have written anything in my journal. It has not been because I have not thought often of my dear ones at home, but from other causes. We have been in some very heavy weather with a great deal of motion to the ship which would have made very unpleasant writing. And, having Mr. Daniels with me and he very sick, I have not felt like writing very much.

I fear it will not be very long before Mr. Daniels will be beyond the cares, sickness and trials of this life. I think it would be almost a miracle if he should live to reach Bombay.

We rounded the Cape of Good Hope on the 20th of February, seventy days out, which was a few days longer than I had expected it to be, but still a fair passage. We are now a little south of the Island of Madagascar and drawing into warm weather again. I expect the change will not

be favorable for Mr. Daniels. The little strength he has left will now, I am afraid, go altogether.

March 17 — Since I last wrote upon this sheet, dear Sarah, time has wrought a melancholy change here. Our passenger, Mr. Daniels, has bid adieu to all the pain and sorrow of this world. He is dead. His spirit has returned to Him who gave it and his body has been committed to an ocean grave. What a sad affliction to his friends who parted with him, no doubt in the firm conviction that this voyage would renovate his health.

On Friday, the 12th, he did not get up but was bolstered up with pillows. I generally took care of him in the night, although he did not require a great deal. But Friday night, I was up with him and about four in the morning, he wanted to be moved to try and get relief but could not tell how he should be moved. He seemed no worse than he had been but I knew he could not last much longer for nature had given out and he was no longer strong, but with disease. He fell asleep soon after sunrise and when he awoke about nine o'clock, he was delirious and did not again have his senses. His voice failed about half-past 11 o'clock. He died the same day, Saturday, March 13th, at 3:30 P.M. and was buried Sunday morning, the 14th, at 9:00 A.M.

For the last eight or ten days, we have had dull, rainy weather and, added to that, a head wind which, of course, made the weather even more unpleasant. But today we have a fair wind and one of the most pleasant days we have had for some time. We are just on the limits of the southeast trade winds. We will not reach Bombay before the 1st of May and perhaps not until after that for we have to go all the way from the equator to Bombay just between the change of the monsoons, which will give us a large share of both winds and calms.

March 21 — Last night was rainy and squally but today is delightful and this is 100 days out. I do not look for less than forty days added to it before we can arrive at Bombay. Last Friday was fourteen weeks since we left Boston. The day before had been rainy but Friday was a beautiful day. At noon Friday, we found ourselves close to the Isle de

France. We had a moderate breeze and sailed just along the eastern side of the island. I assure you, it looked beautiful. The fields of sugar cane looked so green and all around, it appeared so well cultivated. The land rose from the sea in a gentle slope to terminate in the background with mountains in fantastic appearance. The green fields looked so lovely, and it appeared so prosperous. I was quite surprised, for I did not know that the island was so well cultivated. Within the past few years, they have been turning their attention to the raising of sugars and the island is thriving.

March 27 — We have been becalmed for three days and have not made over sixty miles upon our course for the whole of that time. It is enough to try the patience of anyone.

In tropical waters and warm weather, it was important that the *Delhi* make as good time as possible. Days of calm and no wind were of special concern to Captain Barry. Melting ice caused by warm seas meant a rapid depreciation in the value of their cargo. When the ship was in the tropics, her hand-operated pumps were the vessel's most valuable pieces of equipment. They were operated every day to keep the inside of the ship as dry as possible. During calms, everyone on board became fretful. Under such conditions, masters had been known to turn into surly, cross-tempered morons, and some even locked themselves in their cabins, where they took to the bottle. Captain Barry invariably withstood these aggravating circumstances very well, and he never drank anything stronger than tea, no matter what the provocation or occasion might be.

March 29 — We have at last managed to get out of the long calm with which we have been delayed. Yesterday morning, about eight o'clock, a fine trade wind sprang up and we have been making good progress since.

At noon, yesterday, we were about seven miles from the Island of Analega and, at three o'clock we were past it. The land was low and covered with coconut trees. The island is eleven miles long and one mile wide. There was

one place where we could see a considerable village, among the trees, and small native huts. But we could not see a single individual walking upon the beach. I suppose they follow the business of making coconut oil, which is almost the only oil used in India for burning in lamps.

Sunday, April 4 — The day is as calm as can be — not a breath of wind. But it is weather that I expect about here. We are in what sailors call the doldrums — a span of light winds and calms about the region of the equator, between the two trade winds. Yesterday, at noon, we were fourteen miles south of the equator and today we are fifteen miles north of it. So you will perceive, dear Sarah, we have managed to get across that imaginary line and are now in the northern hemisphere. I always seem to feel more at home in north latitude than in south, for that is where I seem to belong. And my dear wife and son and myself are all in the same half of the globe. And that, my love, is a great satisfaction.

As this is Sunday, I think I should write down how I have spent the day. A little after six this morning, I went on deck and had a good bath with a couple of buckets of sea water, and a good scrub with a sponge and two coarse towels. After that, I walked a while on deck, then took breakfast. After that, I read several chapters in the Bible, then whiled away the forenoon as best I could. Dinner came — a plate of pea soup, a side bone of a goose and cranberry sauce, pickles, and so forth. Potatoes don't grow here, so we did without them. We closed off with plum pudding made without milk or eggs. We are 113 days out today but, as you perceive, are not entirely out of fresh food. We have three pigs, four geese and a dozen chickens still left.

The crew of the *Delhi*, it should be noted, ate exceptionally well, especially for the period in which they sailed. The age of rum was passing and the age of canned goods had not arrived. On many other vessels of that era, water, hardtack, molasses and "salt horse" (salted beef) were stand-bys. Nevertheless, a foremast hand on an American East Indiaman was the best paid,

the best fed, and the most competent sailor in the world. Men aboard coasters, fishermen, whalers, and even men-of-war regarded the men who manned the Yankee East India ships as the top dogs of their profession.

Sunday, April 11 — I am really getting pretty tired of light weather and hot sun. We have been eighteen days going only six hundred miles and that, you will agree, is pretty slow progress. I think you would laugh to see me some days, sitting quiet and patiently darning my stockings, a thing I never did before. But you were so kind as to put me up a little work bag in which I found a ball of yarn and needles. I go to work and examine all my stockings before I put them on and wonder that I never did so before. I do not darn as well as you do with them because I do not bestow the time.

Yesterday, we saw three sharks. The shark hook was baited and hung over the stern. It was not long before one of the gentlemen was safely hooked under his jaw with a stout hook attached to a piece of chain. He was hauled on deck. The men took the shark to the gangway, cut him open and what do you suppose was found inside? The feathers of a chicken. About four hours before, when our decks were washed, a chicken was thrown overboard and this was the lucky shark that found that delicious morsel. I mention this to show what powers of digestion sharks must have. In not more than four hours, not a bone, a leg or the least vestige of the chicken was found in him but the feathers.

Before this month has gone by, I hope to be safely in Bombay and in possession of a letter from you. There are so many things I shall wish to hear about. And I shall hear, too, how the Mexican War progresses and how the Whig campaign is getting on, and how many vessels are to be built in Kennebunk this season.

April 15 — Since I last wrote, we have had a fine little breeze and very pleasant weather. It is a very pleasant change after having had such a long spell of calm weather. We are about ten days from Bombay.

After supper at night, the off-duty watch on sailing ships frequently assembled to sing. There was no lack of music on the old square-riggers and some of the men were surprisingly talented. Often, one member of the crew would render the verse of a song, then the whole crew would join in the chorus. All manner of songs were sung. Boat songs, sentimental songs, and such time-honored ones as " The Bay of Biscay," " Poor Tom Bowline," and " Drinking " were especially popular. Captain Barry speaks of this custom as it was practiced on the *Delhi* in the continuation of his journal entry for April 15:

> In the evening, the men sing some very good songs in the forecastle. I like to hear them and tonight, I went on deck and stayed quite a long time to listen.

> *Sunday, April* 18 — This forenoon, I was reading in a book that was a present from you when I heard a violent tramping of feet on deck and running forward from aft. I thought for a moment, what was going on? I jumped up and ran on deck. Just as I got there, I heard the cry " Man overboard!" The man had fallen overboard from the forward part of the ship.

On the sailing ships of the last century, the cry of " Man overboard!" brought more response from the ship's crew than any other that might be sung out during the entire voyage. There was never any need for the added command " All hands on deck!" because immediately upon hearing the ominous cry that a man had gone over the side, every member of the ship's company, from the captain down to the cook and the apprentice boys, rushed on deck. They took their stations without being told; every man knew exactly what move to make, and with clocklike precision, coupled with incredible speed, orders would be given and executed. The man who fell overboard from the forward part of the *Delhi* was extremely fortunate, as Captain Barry's continued account of the incident brings out. Almost instantaneous action on the part of the well-trained crew paid handsome dividends:

The ship's head was instantly stopped and the mate threw the man a rope which he caught just as he was passing the quarter. The gentleman was hauled on board without other injury than a good sousing and considerable fright. His face looked about as white, I reckon, as it ever did before in his life. It was an incident all in the day's duties, although not a very pleasant one. Mr. Barnes said it always put his heart in his throat to hear "man overboard" as he was once overboard himself for three hours before he was hauled aboard again.

The last two or three days, we have been getting along a little better than previously and I am in hopes of getting in in time to send this journal to you by the steamer of May 1st.

April 20 — We have had favorable winds and if they continue, we shall get to Bombay in two or three more days. This noon we were 240 miles from the lighthouse. This morning, we saw a Maldrias boat four or five miles from us, steering towards the coast. I suppose she was from the Maldrias Islands. It is the first vessel of any kind we have seen for over a month and indicates there is someone in this region besides ourselves.

Since dinner, I have shaved and did not spare the whiskers under my chin. "Off with them," I thought, as I do not like to wear whiskers under my chin on shore in warm weather.

April 26 — I think I must improve a few moments and finish up my journal as it is the last I shall be able to write for quite some time. We have arrived in Bombay.

I can hardly tell you, my love, how much trouble and anxiety I have had trying to get into this port. The weather has been so very strong and thick that we could not get any observations. We have been off the port for three days. I was up most of last night, expecting to make land. I need not have been up so much, but I knew that I should not sleep if I were below, and I might as well be on deck. This morning, we made the land but it was so thick and hazy that I thought I could not get hold of the landmarks

to know the harbor. It held very thick all forenoon and we did not get a pilot aboard until four o'clock this afternoon. By then, I had run through the most dangerous parts of the harbor and was almost to the anchorage. I was determined that I should not stand out to sea another day. However, we did get a pilot and here we are, safely at anchor.

I took tea ashore with a gentleman I knew and then came off on board the ship again. I think I shall live ashore while I am here as I have so much business to do. Our anchor was hardly let go before two Parsees [members of a religious sect found throughout India, primarily in Bombay city] came on board, bringing me three letters. One was from Calcutta and one from Captain Parrott on business, and one letter from my own dear Sarah. I could not read them then, but have just done so.

I went on shore, saw the ice folks and had tea, then came off on board about 8:00 P.M., feeling as tired as a dog. I had been on my feet so much, looking through my spy glass, and running into the entrance of the harbor without a chart — I could not get one in Boston before we left — that it made me very anxious and tired.

I sat down and read Captain Parrott's letter on business affairs first and then I read your dear letter and am glad to see that both you and little Willie are continuing well. By the time I had gotten through the letter, I felt perfectly rested, went on deck and walked a little, then came back to finish this journal. . . . .

It's cool and comfortable and I feel perfectly well and have been ever since I left. While in Bombay today, I thought to myself if Sarah was only here how much she would enjoy looking at all the odd things. Riding in a palankeen (a boxlike conveyance borne by poles on the shoulders of four men) and so many things would attract your attention. You were not here, but a good long letter from my dearest, dearest Sarah was in my pocket, and happy was I.

In concluding this journal, I shall say that we have arrived safely after this long passage and I shall forward this journal as soon as I have a favorable opportunity. Now, my dearest love, good night, with one sweet kiss, many times repeated.

Charles

VII

Crystal Blocks of Yankee Coldness

When describing the approach of the *Delhi* to Bombay, Captain Barry had characteristically understated the hazards he had encountered. It had been a treacherous ordeal that warrants some amplification over what he wrote in his journal. Late in the evening of April 22, 1847, the *Delhi* had come up on the lights that marked Bombay Harbor. As it was against port regulations to enter or leave the harbor during the hours of darkness, there had been no alternative except to go out a safe distance from shore, heave to, drop anchor, and wait until morning before proceeding farther. During the night, the weather had changed and the ship had become fog bound.

The first rays of light on the morning of April 26 had found Captain Barry on the *Delhi*'s forecastle head. For three days, the ship had laid at anchor, enveloped in fog and mist off the shore of India in the vicinity of the entrance to Bombay Harbor. A rising barometer during the night had given promise that the ship, at last, might be able to complete her long and tedious voyage. Hoping to pick up the harbor lights as soon as the fog lifted, the captain had been on deck for several hours. But with the breaking of day, the visibility did not improve. Finally, at about nine that morning, Captain Barry, with the aid of his hand-held telescope, had been able to make out the dim outline of Malabar Hill off the starboard bow. The hill, he knew, lay

along the west shore of Bombay Island, close to the harbor entrance. It was about three miles away in a northeasterly direction.

Although he had no harbor chart, Captain Barry knew exactly what to look for along the shore. While standing by, waiting for the weather to clear, he had improved his time by practically memorizing the section on Bombay in a volume called *India Directory, or Directions for Sailing To and From the East Indies, China, New Holland, Cape of Good Hope and Brazil,* which had been published in England in 1835. The captain now knew by heart the channels, tides, harbor buoys, and all prominent landmarks he would encounter when entering the Bombay anchorage. The information in the pilot book would have to serve in lieu of a chart.

By ten, the weather had cleared enough to make it reasonably safe to proceed cautiously, even though the visibility was still very poor. Captain Barry directed Mr. Barnes to get the ship under way. The topsails were set and the anchor raised. Slowly, the *Delhi* commenced to make headway. His telescope always in hand and in nearly constant use, the captain guided the ship past the floating marker and light at the harbor entrance, then safely around Prongs Reef. It was still so foggy that the ship was within a mile of the lighthouse before it was seen by the lookout there. A gun was fired to signal the approach of a vessel, and an open boat put out and headed in the direction of the *Delhi.* Aboard was a harbor pilot who, for a fee of 110 rupees, would take the *Delhi* into the harbor. His boat had a double lanteen rig, which consisted of two sails extended by long yards and hung on short masts. The boat was painted a distinctive red. A black number on the bow identified the pilot who was in the boat.

There are few more impressive sights in the world than the approach to Bombay from the sea. On the left as a ship proceeds up the harbor is the picturesque ancient city and on the right, the palm-fringed shore of the mainland over which the peaks of the Western Ghat Mountains can be seen in the distance. The view was hidden from the men on the *Delhi*

because of fog and haze, but it was there just the same and they would see it later. The pilot guided the ship, through a harbor filled with vessels of every description, to a point near the water-front at the downtown part of the city. Ice ships were given a preferred place to anchor — usually the best berth in the harbor — to facilitate prompt and relatively easy unloading.

A customs-house officer was required to stay on board all foreign vessels during their stay in port. The man assigned to the *Delhi* arrived at the ship's side in a small boat at about the same time that the pilot left. Only a short time before, Mr. Barnes had ordered: " Let go," for the *Delhi*'s anchor to plunge to the bottom. Later, another anchor would be added because ice ships were required by harbor regulations to be double anchored, with thirty fathoms of cable out. The customs official had no sooner climbed the ship's ladder and been greeted by Captain Barry than the Parsees who brought the captain's mail arrived in another boat.

The anchored ship provided no thrill for her crew. There was much for them to do. The vessel had to be made ship-shape, then there would be the cargo to unload. Only after most of the work was done would the crew, one watch at a time, be given a single day and night of liberty ashore during the time that the ship would be in port. Before the day of the ship's arrival was out, they would have to get all the sails down and furled, the rigging separated and hauled taut, and the decks swept clean. But the first order of business after anchoring was to get the longboat lowered to take Captain Barry ashore.

" The boat is ready, sir," called the second mate who, to-gether with the steward, would accompany the captain, the mis-sion of these men being to procure fresh provisions while the captain attended to other business. Captain Barry, dressed in a white cotton coat and trousers and wearing a white sun helmet, eased himself over the side and down the ladder into the boat. The men at the oars pushed away and started to row. The boat glided among the anchored ships to Buna Bandar, a dock-ing place that was lined with many boats — dows, lighters, bunga-low boats, and small merchant vessels of every kind. Sailors were lounging under awnings on their boats, telling yarns, and smoking their hubble-bubble pipes, called hookahs. These were pipes with a long, flexible stem, so arranged that the smoke is cooled by passing through water in a metal container at the end of the stem. Natives on the wharf, clad in light garments, were selling many types of fruit, cakes, toddy rum, carved wood, and curios to those sailors who had a few annas to spend.

When the trio from the *Delhi* stepped out of their longboat, the mate and the steward were besieged by vendors of fruits and vegetables who wanted their patronage. Others tried to thrust all manner of things for sale upon the men — fans, carved boxes, pipes, sugar cane, and colored calicoes. Captain Barry pushed through the small throng, leaving the mate and the steward behind to make their purchases then wait for him at the boat. He made his way up the street to the Customs House and then to the office of Frederick Tudor's Bombay representative, where he took tea. About him lay the city proper with its mercantile houses, hotels, shops, bazaars, grand old ruins, palaces of the nabobs, coffeehouses, and even a first-rate theater.

The following day, April 27, Captain Barry went ashore again to visit the office of the American Consul and to complete the final arrangements for unloading the *Delhi*'s cargo. He posted his letters, paying particular attention to the very long letter — his personal journal of four months — that was addressed to Sarah in Maine. The steamer that carried what was known as the "overland mail" departed from Bombay on the first of every month. It sailed through the Arabian and Red Seas to Suez from where the mail was taken by camel caravan to Alexandria on the Mediterranean. Here, the mail was put on board another steamer and carried by way of the Strait of Gibraltar to England. This service, which required forty-five days, had been started in 1838. When the Suez Canal was opened in 1869, the time for a letter to reach England from India was reduced to thirty days. Mail for the United States was transferred at Liverpool to the *Great Western,* or one of the Cunard steamers, and required another fifteen days to reach its destination.

123

On the *Delhi*'s third day in port, wide, flat native boats that served as lighters commenced coming out to the ship to unload cargo. Their large triangular sails billowed in the breeze as they approached Captain Barry's vessel. Just as collision seemed inevitable, the skipper of the craft would put down his helm and swing his boat around to come neatly alongside the *Delhi*. He would let his big sail flap in the wind all the time that cargo was being transferred.

The *Delhi* was carrying a divided cargo, half being consigned to Bombay and half to Calcutta, which would be delivered later. The apples — one hundred barrels of them — were unloaded first. These were a rare treat in that tropical climate and they brought a very fancy price. Having been packed in the hold with the ice, they were as fresh and firm as the day they had been picked in the New England orchard where they had grown.

The *Delhi* had been at anchor four days before the first ice was taken ashore. The hand-operated windlass device that had been used for loading the ice at Charlestown had been brought along. It was set up on deck and the two tracks with their gigs that traveled up and down in opposite directions were lowered like gangways to the bottom of the native lighter, which tied up at the side of the ship. As the ice cakes had to be pulled from the hold with a block and tackle, one cake at a time, the unloading process went slowly. It was slowed even more every time a loaded lighter had to be replaced by an empty one, because the tracks on which the gigs operated had to be pulled up, then lowered again. Once it had received all the ice it could carry, a lighter made for shore with all possible haste so no more ice than necessary would be lost by melting. When the ice reached the icehouse, it was packed in rice chaff. From the time the ice was first loaded aboard the *Delhi* at Charlestown until it was finally packed away in the icehouse at Bombay, the loss by melting amounted to about one-third of the original weight of the cargo. Yet, ice was such a precious commodity in India that it made a profitable cargo in spite of the loss.

To the native workmen on the lighters that were unloading the *Delhi,* ice was no novelty and they were used to handling it. But this had not always been the case. Back in 1833, when Tudor had sent his first shipment of ice to Calcutta, the natives who touched the "crystal blocks of Yankee coldness," as one person dubbed them, had drawn their hands away in imagined pain. They had cried out, wrapped their hands in a fold of their robe and run away, firmly believing that the ice had burned them. One Parsee native was said to have asked: "How this ice make grow in your country? Him grow on tree? Him grow on shrub? How he make grow?" Indignant natives who had left their ice sitting in the sun returned to the icehouse to demand their money back after their ice had melted. A Parsee had accosted the mate of Tudor's first ice-carrying ship to Calcutta, the *Tuscany.* "Mr. Mate," he had complained, "me buy one piece ice of you. Somebody make steal him. Me no find. Me want more piece of ice." The ice, of course, had melted.

The only ice that had been seen in Calcutta prior to 1833 was some frozen ooze from the plain of the Hooghly River. It was made by skimming surface ice from water that seeped into unglazed pots that were placed in reed-lined pits overnight.

For once, Frederick Tudor had not been faced with having to raise the money to build an icehouse. The English inhabitants of Calcutta had offered to construct one if Tudor would deliver the ice. "The idea of having the purest ice at three halfpence a pound the whole year round instead of having the Hooghly slush for only six weeks during the coldest weather at four pence the pound was irresistible," a contemporary Calcutta historian had recorded.

Tudor accepted the terms offered him and sent the *Tuscany* under the command of Captain Littlefield to Calcutta with one hundred eighty tons of ice. "As soon as you have arrived at Latitude twelve degrees north," he told Captain Littlefield, "you have carried ice as far south as it has ever been carried before and your ship becomes a discovery ship. And, as such, I feel confident you will do everything for the eventual success of the

undertaking, being in charge, as you are, of the first ship that has ever carried ice to the East Indies."

After sailing through the tropics, the *Tuscany* had landed with almost two-thirds of her chilly cargo still unmelted. The first shipment did not show a profit. Nevertheless, the Indian ice trade soon became a pecuniary success. The poverty in the country made it difficult for Tudor to establish a wide market for the ice, at first, although cold drinks from the beginning were in great demand by the Anglo-Indian community along the Calcutta waterfront. The arrival of a New England ice ship became the occasion for genial merriment. The captains from Boston moored their ships near the banks of the Hooghly River where they played host with drinks mixed "Yankee fashion" to the officers from the other vessels anchored at the port.

The export of ice to India steadily increased in volume and importance. It enabled Boston to hold the key to rich and extensive commerce with Calcutta at a time when the trade might have otherwise dwindled to extinction. In fact, the ice trade came just in time to save New England's East India commerce from ruin. The American importing business from India had been cut to the roots by the protective tariff of 1816, and a few years later Massachusetts mills were making cotton goods of sufficient quality, quantity, and variety to kill the demand for Indian fabrics that had existed in Federalist days. Until the ice trade came along, a precarious foothold had been held in India by Boston merchants only by exporting such "notions" as spiced Penobscot (Maine) salmon, cod tongues and sounds, coarse glassware, sperm candles, and Cape Cod Glauber salt.

Between 1836 and 1850, the Boston ice trade was extended to every large port in the Far East. By 1840 Tudor had opened icehouses in both Madras and Bombay. In contrast to the icehouses in the United States, which were like big double-walled wooden barns, the Indian icehouses were ornate affairs built of stone. The one at Madras, for instance, was square in shape and about three stories high. It had a circular rotunda on the

waterside facade, which was supported by pilasters of Palladian design.

The regularity of the ice shipments to India was fairly good, but when there was a break in the pattern, the English residents became very unhappy. At one time, a shipwreck caused the Bombay icehouse to run out of ice. The incident was considered so important that the arrival of the first ice ship after the interruption was enthusiastically heralded by headlines in a Bombay newspaper.

With a profitable type of cargo now available to fill the holds of their ships on the Boston to India voyage, Boston merchants soon found new East Indian products to replace the fabrics that had been imported from Bombay and Calcutta in the earlier days. " East India goods " between 1835 and the American Civil War came to mean water buffalo hides, jute, indigo and other dye stuffs, linseed and shellac, saltpeter and gunny cloth. The gunny cloth, in particular, almost always found a ready American market. It was sent south for bailing cotton, and after it had been made up into gunny bags, it was shipped to the corn growers of the west for sacking their corn. The ice trade during the mid-1840 period increased to such proportions that Frederick Tudor was able to pay off a debt of a quarter of a million dollars that he had accumulated during his earlier ice-exporting experiments.

At Calcutta, Madras, and Bombay, ice had become a well-established business by the time the *Delhi* arrived at the last-named port. Nothing at all was thought of the lighters that plied back and forth in the harbor, carrying the ice they were unloading from the ship. Day after day, six days a week, for about two weeks, the work went on.

On Sunday, native " bumboats " came out to the anchored ships in the harbor. They carried almost every conceivable kind of article that might please a sailor's fancy, offering to exchange their wares for whatever the crews had to offer. They would take books, boots, clothing, or anything else that the sailors found handy to trade. " Changee for changee, John,"

was the cry as the bumboats went from ship to ship. The going price was a dollar a pair for boots, or for a song book and a Bible together. Old clothing had a similar value. In return, these cruising storekeepers offered dates fresh from the tree, ginger from China, silks, fans, sandalwood boxes, ivory carvings, needles, liquor, flags, monkeys, coconut oil, cheap perfume, toys, ostrich feathers, and many other articles. When a bumboat drew alongside the *Delhi,* her sailors would climb down the ship's ladder to go aboard the boat and dicker with the owner. In many a quiet New England home, the ever-present " what-not " displayed curiosities that some member of the family had obtained from one of these floating East India shopmen.

While the *Delhi* lay in port, there were many simple pleasures that the crew devised for themselves. The long evenings offered the ship's company a chance for relaxing aboard the vessel when the day's work was done. After supper, there would be a grand cleaning-up. Every member of the crew took a salt-water bath and put on clean clothes. Usually, an impromptu " band " from the crew would play familiar songs. One of the sailors had an accordion and another had a flute. A third had a tin whistle, and a drummer beat on a drum that had been made by stretching a native goat hide over a round cheese box. The combined effect of these instruments was pleasing to both the performers and the audience. Sometimes, there was a " master of ceremonies " who saw to it that every man and boy among the crew had their bit to do. One after another, the men were called upon to sing some particular song, then the whole company would join in the chorus. Of course, there was no printed music, so the tune was apt to be a little modified at times and some liberties were taken with the words. But the men thought that the singing was the finest ever, chiefly because they, themselves, were producing it.

As the time for the *Delhi* to leave Bombay drew near, the port and starboard watches were given their day of shore liberty. Most of the sailors who crowded into the *Delhi*'s longboat to be taken ashore wore a fathom of wide black ribbon wrapped around

their heads for a hat, a black silk scarf tied about their neck in a neat sailor's knot, white duck trousers, and black pumps.

Some of the men, as might well be imagined, lost both their heads and their money not long after they reached dry land. They fell into the hands of unscrupulous tavern-keepers who were only too willing to accept their hard-earned wages for whatever form of dissipation suited their individual fancy.

Others of the crew made the most of their time in the city. For eight annas, they could hire a crude type of buggy drawn by a mule, which carried them safely around Bombay and out into the country on a sightseeing tour. The tour lead them past palaces and temples, by cemeteries with tall columns at the entrance and ghostly headstones within, through groves of coconut trees and fields of bright flowers, past huge banyan trees with many trunks, and along fields of rice and cane. The streets and roads along which the touring sailors rode were filled with people on foot — Parsee natives, whites, pagans, Jews both in and out of bondage, crippled beggars, and handsome Hindu girls carrying heavy jars of water on their heads. Occasionally, some wealthy European would pass in a palankeen. The box-like conveyances with a reclining couch on the inside and shutters on the outside were borne on the shoulders of natives who jogged along at a dogtrot, perspiration streaming down their faces. They often sang chants as they trotted through the streets.

Nearly three weeks after the ship had arrived, the *Delhi* was made ready to sail from Bombay. Half the ice and half the Baldwin apples still remained in the hold. On the fourteenth of May, the day before the sailing date, a fresh supply of pigs, a few goats, a number of ducks, and two dozen hens were brought on board and placed in the pens and hatches on the deck. The water barrels were filled with fresh water, and baskets of fresh vegetables were piled near the forecastle. Just before dark, the carpenter sealed the hatches.

As early as possible the next morning, Captain Barry cleared the ship at the Customs House. The harbor pilot boarded the ship, and at 10:00 A.M., Mr. Barnes gave the command, " Man the windlasses," to start the noisy operation of getting the an-

chors up. Then the sails were raised. They billowed out in the wind and the *Delhi* gathered headway as she proceeded out of Bombay Harbor. A brief stop was made near the lighthouse while the pilot climbed down the ladder to his waiting little red boat. By noon, the *Delhi* was at sea on her way to Calcutta.

The voyage south, around the southern tip of India, then north again to Calcutta was uneventful but slow. The many calm days were frustrating to both Captain Barry and the crew. As the water temperature in the Gulf of Mannar and Palk Strait between India and Ceylon was about 80°, the slow progress was neither good for the cargo nor the disposition of the vessel's captain. For a while, during one four-day spell of calm weather in the Bay of Bengal, the ice melted so rapidly that the ship's pumps had to be manned every day.

On July 6, 1847, approximately seven weeks after making her departure from Bombay, the *Delhi* finally arrived at Sand Heads at the mouth of the Hooghly River, eighty miles south of Calcutta. At the floating lighthouse at Sand Heads, Captain Barry took a river pilot aboard. Slowly the *Delhi* made her way up the channels of the Hooghly River to Diamond Harbor, about a third of the way up the river toward Calcutta. There, the ship stopped to take on a customs-house officer who would accompany the *Delhi* the rest of the way. Captain Barry also engaged a steamboat to tow his vessel from this point on. It was not specially designed for this use. Nevertheless, it served the purpose admirably, which was fortunate for Captain Barry. Before the tow steamer had become available, it had sometimes taken as long as two weeks under adverse conditions for a sailing ship to beat her way up the Hooghly River to Calcutta. The seventy-five dollars per day that the tow steamer cost was worth it.

The trip from Diamond Harbor to Calcutta required the better part of a day and a night. Cautiously, the steamer with the *Delhi* in tow proceeded upriver, around Hooghly Point. During the hours of darkness, the cries of tigers and other wild animals could be heard clearly nearby as the ship passed close to the tangled jungles along the banks of the lower part of the river. The sun had come up by the time the *Delhi* passed

Garden Reach, an anchorage three miles below Calcutta. On arrival at Calcutta, Captain Barry had the anchor dropped in a manner that positioned the ship as one of a long line of vessels that were moored along the river bank, parallel to the city's waterfront. It was a dangerous anchorage because strong tidal currents often formed whirlpools, called bores, which sometimes fouled a ship's ground tackle.

Ashore, Captain Barry found four letters awaiting him from Sarah, one from Captain Parrott, and several from other people. He contacted Frederick Tudor's agent and arranged for the ice to be unloaded. The operation, which was conducted much as it had been at Bombay, required ten days. The apples were placed on the local market immediately. It was said that those apples that eventually reached China sold in that country at a price equal to their weight in silver.

Of necessity, the *Delhi* had to remain at Calcutta for about eight weeks. After the ice had been unloaded and taken ashore, all the sawdust that had been used for dunnaging had to be removed, and the hold had to be dried out by leaving all ports and hatches open except when it rained. This took a long time. Captain Barry, who stayed at a Calcutta hotel during this period, was busy all the while contracting for a suitable cargo to carry back to Boston.

As soon as the ship was unloaded and cleaned, the crew were discharged, save for the two mates, Mr. Barnes and Mr. Cabot, the steward, and the three apprentice boys. But having to leave the ship at a foreign port did not bother the crew, as this was customary. At the American consul's office, they could sign up and reship for almost immediate departure on another vessel bound for home, or almost any other port, at practically any time they wanted to leave Calcutta.

The mates, the steward, and the three boys lived aboard the *Delhi,* where either one mate or the other was always on duty to be responsible for the ship. Ordinarily, the cook would not have been discharged. Captain Barry later described in his journal how it came about that he had been this time.

Even the old ebony cook had to be discharged. He used to get sulky, and he and the steward could not get along together. I thought it was best to discharge one of them, as you know how it is when two girls [servants] in the kitchen are always bickering with each other. The sooner you get rid of one of them, the better. And, consequently, I paid the old cook off and he was glad to go. I managed to get another in his place the same day. He came aboard and cooked for two or three days — got his advance wages and went ashore a day, to spend it. And, being a regular drunkard, he fell down, broke three of his ribs, and was sent to the hospital. Of course, I had to get another cook and picked up the one we have now. I have not discovered any traits of character in him, as yet, which would make it worth while to mention him further.

Captain Barry bargained in Calcutta for return freight much as a modern housewife might shop from place to place for household goods. In due course, he completed negotiations with the Calcutta mercantile export firms of Babu-Rajkissen-Mitter, and Jamsetjee and Jeejeebhoy and Company. On or before the twentieth of August, these two companies, between them, were to furnish a mixed cargo for the *Delhi*, consisting of saltpeter, cowhides, goatskins, shellac, dye, linseed, gunny cloth, and jute, jute being an easily spun fiber used for making burlap. The goods would be crated, boxed, baled, or barreled, as might be required, and delivered aboard the ship by the specified date.

The *Delhi* was due to sail from Calcutta on August 22, 1847. About two weeks before this, a messenger called upon Captain Barry with the following letter:

Spencer's Hotel
Calcutta

Captain Barry

Dear Sir:

I have not had the time to call around and see you, so pray excuse this note, instead. I made up my mind this morning to return with you on the *Delhi,* provided we can agree as to conditions.

First, then, for the sum of $300, you are to take me from Calcutta to Boston in the ship *Delhi*. I cannot but think that $300 is too much for a passage home in your ship, considering the small accommodations, as I can obtain a passage in any one of the fine Green ships for 800 rupees, including wines.

What think you? In the *Saxonville*, I could have returned for $200, but many times that sum would not have tempted me to sail in her again. Moreover, dear captain, I am to take one or two monkeys with me if I should be disposed, which I promise shall cause you no trouble.

If you can find time, please answer this by my messenger who will wait for your reply.

With my respects to yourself,

Your obedient servant,

/s/ Frederick Fitzgerald

Captain Barry replied by offering to carry one or two monkeys free of charge, but he would not reduce the cost of the passage to Boston below three hundred dollars. These terms were accepted by Mr. Fitzgerald. The captain also sold passage on the *Delhi* to a missionary couple, a Mr. and Mrs. Cape, and their twelve-year-old son.

Ten days before the sailing date, Captain Barry commenced hiring another crew. He went to the American consul's office, where he almost had to push his way through the dozen or more seamen who were waiting outside, each trying to get a berth on a homeward bound vessel. On hearing the captain's story, the consul called in the waiting sailors. "I want men. Must have them," Captain Barry told them. "Do any of you want to ship to Boston in the *Delhi*?" To those he accepted from the ones who volunteered, he added, "Will you please sign the articles and go aboard today?" In two days time, Captain Barry had the eighteen men he needed.

As the sailing date drew near, cargo came out to the *Delhi* faster every day. Wide native boats swept down the muddy river to pull alongside the ship. The natives on the boats tossed sacks of linseed, bales of gunny cloth and jute, bundles of hides and barrels of dye on a staging from where the goods were loaded on the ship through a porthole by four men of the *Delhi*'s new crew. Other crew members lowered the various items into the hold where they were packed away in rows. When the hold was filled, the between-decks space was loaded. Last to be brought on board and placed in the pig sty, sheep pen, and poultry hatches on the deck was the fresh food supply for the four months' voyage that lay ahead. From the inventory that Captain Barry gave later in his journal, there were fifteen dozen ducks, eight dozen hens, two dozen geese, eight dozen pigeons, twelve pigs, four sheep, and two goats. There were also many other fresh food items, including one hundred pumpkins. "I always like to supply my ship decently and have no stint, without being either stingy or extravagant," the captain wrote.

The problems involved in getting the *Delhi* to sea can be told best by quoting from his journal:

> Thursday, the 21st, at noon, the ship was completely loaded but there were the hatches to be caulked down, the decks cleaned up and the ship to be cleared at the Customs House. As my passengers would not get on board until Friday and I could clear the Customs House then, I decided to take the ship out of mooring to drop down the river about three miles to a better anchorage at Garden Reach. In doing so, the *Delhi* met with an accident which caused some detention. The tides are fearfully strong during the freshets, which cause strong eddies and make a ship unmanageable. To avoid this, ships drop this distance below Calcutta to Garden Reach by letting the anchor and chain lay upon the bottom, dragging, which keeps the ship's head to the tide so that she can be steered by the rudder.
>
> As we were dropping down in this manner, our anchor caught a heavy chain and anchor which were laid down for mooring the large overland steamers [i.e., the steamers carrying the overland mail to Suez]. We could not, for a whole day, get clear of it. I was in continued anxiety while the ship was in the river, caught on the chain, as I knew she was liable any moment, by taking a bad shear across the strong tide, to do herself much injury. The damage she

might have sustained would have caused us to go back to town for two months or more while being repaired in Calcutta. But we did get clear and eventually got safely at anchor.

There was not time Friday to clear the Customs House and the passengers had not come on board. The Customs House closed at noon on Saturday for the weekend. If I did not clear the ship by then, we could have done nothing until Monday and we would not have been able to get the ship started down the river until Tuesday.

I drove with all my might and got through the Customs House just five minutes before it closed. Mr. Cape and his wife and child came aboard with their baggage Sunday morning. Some of my crew disobeyed orders and managed to get off the ship on Saturday night. When they came back from town early Sunday, they were in a miserable state from their exertion on shore. I had to put four of them who were very refractory in irons, although two days later they thought better of their conduct and I let them out of their handcuffs.

The pilot came on board and I got the ship out of her moorings. Then I went back to Calcutta in a native boat to finish closing my business. I told the mate to let the ship drop down the river with the tide and I would join the ship later by overtaking her with the boat. These native boats are large and are called " bungalow boats." They have a kind of house on the after part of them with windows and blinds on each side, and they have a seat on each side that is long enough for one person to lie down upon. The seats are cushioned. About seven or eight boatmen to row and sail are attached to each boat.

Sunday afternoon, I called with my boat at Dr. Huffnagle's at Garden Reach to take on board Mr. Fitzgerald, my other passenger, who, during the latter part of his stay at Calcutta, had lived with them. I had made arrangements to call for him there. I spent a few moments at the house during which time the boatmen were getting Mr. Fitzgerald's luggage on board, including many things, among which was a live monkey. After all was ready, we bid Dr. Huffnagle and his wife, who stood on the embankment, good-bye. We

left Garden Reach about an hour before sunset with the tide and a light wind in our favor.

About one or two o'clock Monday morning, being about half asleep, I heard the boat go alongside a ship. I at first thought it was ours, but it proved to be a Liverpool ship called the *Hurra Hendersen* that had left town about the same time the *Delhi* did. A person on deck said he had seen an American ship astern of them about five o'clock and he had not seen her pass and did not think that she had. It left the matter in uncertainty, and I came to the conclusion that my boatmen had got asleep and passed our ship without seeing her. It would be somewhat remarkable if a Hindu did not get asleep at every opportunity as well as to take a smoke of his hubble bubble pipe whenever he could.

I thought the safest plan was to keep on down the river as far as Diamond Harbor, where there was a semaphore telegraph station and ascertain if our ship had passed. We reached there about daylight. There is a house there where the customs-house officers live. They join a ship going up and leave the ship coming down at this place. The super-intendent of the station invited us to take breakfast with them and we accepted. The Harbor Master of Calcutta whom I had seen in town was there. He was expecting his wife out from England on one of the large packet ships called the *Prince of Wales* and he had come down to meet the ship, which was already overdue. Our pilot who was on board the *Delhi* was also expecting his wife and her sister on the same ship. The people out here who have English wives have to send them home occasionally to recover their health as they cannot stand the climate.

Well, after we had eaten breakfast, the tide turned to run up, and we went on board our boat to proceed up the river again to meet our ship. We got on board about noon and glad enough to get there after spending a rather un-comfortable night upon the river. Mr. Fitzgerald was not very well, having a little cold and fever. You may imagine that we had rather crowded conditions in our small accom-modations on the *Delhi*. There was myself, four passengers and our officers, the pilot and a leadsman, and the customs-house officer. We anchored the ship a little below Diamond

Harbor about five o'clock in the afternoon and the customs-house officer got off.

The last day that the pilot was on board, we saw two vessels coming up the river just before sunset, towing up by steamer. We pronounced them packets and one of them the *Prince of Wales*. I was joking the pilot about it and told him I supposed we could have the liberty of looking as the ships passed. I told him I would pick out his wife. He said that he expected that was more than he could do, as the ship was full of passengers and troops.

The pilot of the *Prince of Wales* had told our pilot's wife and sister, I suppose, what pilot was on the *Delhi*. Fitzgerald, myself and the pilot stood on the forecastle head, looking at the other ship with glasses as she came near. She was full of passengers, but in a moment, two white handker-chiefs from her deck began to flutter in the breeze. The two pilots exchanged salutations as the vessels passed. Then I told our pilot which of the two ladies who waved handker-chiefs was his wife and where she stood.

I knew the wife by her keeping her handkerchief to her face after the ships had passed. I could imagine what her feelings were. She had met her husband, seen him, heard the sound of his voice, but without the power to exchange one word or to give him one embrace. It was more than her overcharged heart could bear, and she sought relief in allow-ing the pearly drops to flow from her eyes. And it was by this that I knew which was his wife.

We discharged the pilot at the Sand Heads lightship about three o'clock in the morning on Thursday, August 28th, and I once more got the ship into my own hands. I pointed her prow towards home with a happy feeling and with great relief to my mind. By daylight, a good breeze had sprung up to carry us on our way down the Bay of Bengal.

VIII

Homeward Bound

All the long way out from Boston and down and across the Atlantic Ocean to the Cape of Good Hope, " around the corner " and up to Bombay and Calcutta, the thoughts of the permanent members of the *Delhi*'s crew had been on home. From Captain Barry to the apprentice boys, they had dreamed of the day they would be headed back to their home port. This was also true for many of the new crew members who had joined the ship at Calcutta, for they, too, had originally come from New England cities or towns. All through the days that had stretched into weeks and the weeks that had dragged into months since they had departed from the United States, nearly everyone on board the *Delhi* had anticipated the time they would be homeward bound. And now they were.

The route of the *Delhi* on the return voyage was somewhat different from the one that had been followed on the outbound voyage. The direction of the prevailing winds and currents caused the difference. After rounding the Cape of Good Hope, the homebound ship sailed northwest across the South Atlantic to a point off the eastern tip of Brazil in the vicinity of Natal. Then, still proceeding northwest, the ship passed just to the east of the West Indies and the Bahama Islands. When about opposite Cape Kennedy, Florida, the course changed to almost due north to reach Cape Cod by the most direct route. And once the *Delhi* rounded Cape Cod, there was only Massachusetts Bay to cross before the ship entered Boston Harbor.

As in the case of the outward-bound voyage, the home voyage of the *Delhi* is best described by Captain Barry himself, in the personal journal he kept for Sarah:

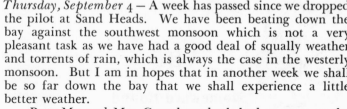

Thursday, September 4 — A week has passed since we dropped the pilot at Sand Heads. We have been beating down the bay against the southwest monsoon which is not a very pleasant task as we have had a good deal of squally weather and torrents of rain, which is always the case in the westerly monsoon. But I am in hopes that in another week we shall be so far down the bay that we shall experience a little better weather.

Poor Mr. and Mrs. Cape have both had to come to the confession that they are really sea sick. It has been so rough this past day or two that she has been more sick than he. Mr. Cape and his wife are both invalids, or, in fact, worn out missionaries and are both as quiet as lambs. All of their energies seem to be gone and yet he has only been twelve years in Ceylon, and is only forty-three years of age. His wife, I should think, is about the same, and their boy is twelve. Mr. Cape remarked to me this noon that this is the first time in ten years that he has been out of the tropics.

Today, I got my first sick patient since leaving Calcutta. He was one of the gentlemen who had gone into town without my authority on the night before the ship started down the river from Garden Reach. He has loved some fair lady, not too long nor too well — but unwisely, and so well that he has received his ailment as an indelible impression of her kindness. I reckon it will take not too long to place the gentleman in better circumstances. I hope his experiences will make him a better man. But I fear that the dangers past will be too readily forgotten to improve the steps he will take the next time he goes ashore in the future.

September 15 — The last two days have been very good weather. This morning it was perfectly calm and the sea as smooth as could be. Soon after breakfast, I was on the forecastle head when I saw something floating in the

water, the ship then only moving at about a knot an hour. I took the spy glass and saw it was a large turtle. As we came near, I asked the mate if he intended to try to get him. I told him he might take four hands in the boat and see if they could catch him. Sailors are always ready for any such fun as that, and they jumped to clear away the quarter boat. When, lo, there was another great turtle and larger, floating by the side of the ship.

In a few minutes, the boat was down and away they went for the first turtle. They soon had him into the boat. Then they pulled away for the other. He saw the boat and made signs of having a dive all to himself — but the men grabbed hold of one of his flippers and soon had him in the boat. And in less than half an hour, we had two fine turtles on board that should weigh from one hundred to one hundred forty pounds each. As soon as we had got the boat hoisted up, a little breeze sprang up which has continued since.

September 20 — I must tell you, dear Sarah, that I am comfortable as one can be at sea. I have a good crew and officers, a good cook and steward and my passengers appear to be agreeable and pleasant. Our ship is rather overfull and crowded but we all get along very well. Our passengers are all looking forward to our progress and calculating the different parallels to be crossed during the passage. First, the equator, then the Cape of Good Hope, and St. Helena on the other side, then the equator again, and after that, the parallel of Bermuda — then comes Cape Cod and, lastly, the getting of a pilot to get us into Boston.

Both of the turtles that we caught died, one after the other, in a most unexpected and unaccountable manner. I had always supposed that they could hardly be killed. But we lost them both and, as usual, some of our live stock have died. But we generally calculate for them to go pretty fast when we first get out. In three weeks, we have lost about twenty ducks and hens and a pig.

September 24 — This morning we had an exciting incident for a few minutes and I will relate it. It was about eight o'clock. The wind was blowing a good breeze and some sea was on. I was sitting at the cabin table, looking over an

old newspaper, while the steward was cleaning up after breakfast. He was nearly done when I heard a great noise and carrying-on, on the forward part of the ship. I jumped up and rushed to the deck. I sung out what was the matter? "A man overboard," was the reply.

At the first cry of trouble, the off-duty watch had appeared on deck to man their stations as if by a miracle, so quick did they get there. The ship was on the port tack at the time. The mate, Mr. Barnes, ordered the starboard watch to weather the main braces. The second mate, Mr. Cabot, slacked away the lee braces. As the yards swung around, Mr. Barnes yelled to the helmsman to put the helm down to bring the ship around into the wind. This put the mainsail flat aback to receive the wind from the opposite side. The effect was to stop the *Delhi* dead in her tracks.

A man was ordered to the mizzentop to keep a sharp lookout for the unfortunate sailor. While this was going on, Mr. Barnes supervised the port watch in getting a boat into the water, which was no simple matter as all of the *Delhi*'s boats were chocked up and securely lashed to keep them from being damaged in heavy seas. Everything happened so fast that the ship had been stopped and the boat made almost ready to be put over the side by the time Captain Barry reached the deck. His journal related the rest of the incident:

When I got on deck, the ship's helm had been put down and she came around to the wind and deadened her way through the water. I jumped on the taffrail and saw the fellow about forty or fifty feet astern. We threw over a small box that was lying near and I saw that the fellow had got hold of it. The quarter boat was cleared away and low-ered down. And in just twenty-one minutes from the time the man fell overboard, we had him back on board again. The same little careless boy had been overboard once before in a river. But he got no further injury than a good ducking and a fright. This makes two persons that have tumbled overboard this voyage, and as long as I have been to sea, they are the only instances I have ever witnessed.

I have a new patient who is pretty sick with a bowel complaint, and I cannot seem to make much impression upon his complaint. I don't know how it is, but I always seem to get a pretty good share of doctor's duty to perform, much against my inclination because it is not my regular business.

September 30 — A year seems a great while to be so far away from those I love. I must say that I do not like India voyages. I have always said and think that a man will grow old faster in the India trade than he will by freighting to Europe. I judge from myself, and I can perceive that I have changed a good deal. I have grown as thin as a hatchet and my hair is nearly all fallen from the top of my head. Being in this constant hot weather, perspiring so much all the time, it is no wonder that a person gets thin and poor.

The other day, I set my watch to Kennebunk time and have it hanging at the head of my berth and running. Not infrequently, I look at it to see what o'clock it is with my dear Sarah, and I try to picture what you are doing. I usually store my watch away in my trunk when at sea, to save the trouble of winding it, but now I think that I will keep it running on Kennebunk time until I get home.

October 5 — I think that I must write a few lines today to my dearest, dearest Sarah, and if I can find nothing to write about, I can tell her how dearly I love her, how much I think of her and how much I would give to be by her side, knowing that such a thing cannot be because many, many weary miles still intervene. But the last few days have been fine and pleasant and we are gradually lessening the distance which separates us. I long, my dear Sarah, to be again at home, freed from the cares of the ship, seated by your side and enjoying your society, with our divided care of little Willie. I have for the second or third time today been looking at the miniature of my dear little wife.

I sometimes sit on deck and enjoy watching the pigeons we have on board. Their coop is open and they have the privilege of coming out as much as they like. They like right well to stretch themselves out in the sun and jump into a little basin of water to clean their feathers. They are perfectly tame and remain aft, in the vicinity of the coop. You will ask me what do we want with these pigeons. Why, my dear Sarah, we want them to eat. We want to broil and make pot pies of them.

October 11 — My patient that I had sick with dysentery is still sick. I succeeded in arresting his disease but he has not got up and a day or two back, he had a slight fever. He says he was never sick before in his life. He was a stout fellow and you would be surprised to see how he has become broken down.

This morning, a fellow came to me to extract a tooth for him. I invariably tell them that I don't extract teeth, and the reason I will not do it for them is that it is a thing of no positive necessity. They knew before they came aboard my ship that the tooth was bad, and it is their business to get a dentist and pay for him extracting it, out of the money they would otherwise spend on rum and prostitution.

Later, the steward asked if he might take the instruments from the chest. He said that he had pulled teeth before and the man wanted him to extract it. I said yes, that if he was willing to extract the tooth, he could have the instruments to do so. Soon after, the steward came to me with a molar tooth in his hand and a very small portion of the jaw bone adhering to it. I told him that it would do no harm and sent him off.

October 14 — This morning we discovered a small brig astern of us and evidently gaining on us. About one o'clock, she came up with us and passed a very short distance from us. I expected she was going to speak us but there was some sea on and I suppose the skipper did not because these small vessels are generally rather timid of being near a large one unless it is quite smooth. I read her name with the glass. *Mezeppa*. She is probably bound from the Isle of France to the Cape of Good Hope. She could not be out more than two or three days.

The *Mezeppa* had some large plants in tubs sitting on deck and several passengers. One of them was a lady. She was sitting upon the deck in an armchair, holding an umbrella over her to keep her complexion from tanning.

It looked comfortable to see a lot of passengers on board another ship at sea. If the brig is bound for the Cape of Good Hope, I suppose she will report us. In sixteen or eighteen more days, I hope we shall round the Cape ourselves.

October 16 — My patient that I have had on hand for a long time and who has been considerably better, seems to have taken a change and is now on the retrograde, and getting worse. He has been so long this way now that I fear I shall not be able to check his complaint although I shall do all in my power to do so.

I have just laid aside my pen to take my meridian observations of the sun at noon. Now the steward says, "Dinner is ready, sir," and I must off.

(Later) I will tell you what I had for dinner and you may judge for yourself if we eat well enough. First, we had mock turtle soup, then a fore shoulder of roast pork with applesauce. Pickles, potatoes and then we had tapioca pudding assisted along by a small piece of cheese, and that ended our humble meal.

I employed myself this afternoon cutting out a small sail and cleaning my pistols, which have not been cleaned in a long time. This noon, one of the sailors caught a couple of large bonita fish. For some nights past, we have discovered that rats have been making some havoc among our poultry and this morning, I set the carpenter to work making some boards to fit over the slats of the coops so they could be closed up before dark. And I told him to fix some rat traps and see that they were in order. At dark, the traps were set and just before eight o'clock we found our traps had been sprung, but the tenant of one cage escaped. The other trap caught a rat.

October 21 — Oh dear, dear. Here we are, my dear Sarah, for two whole days, almost becalmed. Our breeze vanished quite suddenly and rather unexpectedly to me. We were left in the doldrums with light, baffling airs. That means we have done very little in the way of getting along for the past two days. And it makes me a little impatient, for I am anxious to get home to the ones I love. You know, dearest, that loving you as much as I do, a year is such a long while to be separated from you.

My poor patient whom I have had for so long, I fear will never get well. He grows worse instead of better and I have done for him all that I know how to do.

October 26 — Since I last wrote in my journal, my poor patient who has been so long sick with dysentery has gone to his long home. He died yesterday and was buried a few hours afterward. He was one of the best men we had, or appeared to be so. He had sailed with the mate before who says he was a first rate man. He belonged to one of the Shetland Isles at the north of Scotland, where I suppose he has a mother living as he wished his things sold and the proceeds sent to her. I believe he was a steady man and no doubt was of some assistance to her, whose tears of sorrow are yet to be shed for perhaps an only son.

October 28 — Well, my dear Sarah, we have almost got to the Cape of Good Hope, but not quite. We are so near around that we shall probably be so tomorrow. Yesterday we had a gale from the eastward with a very liberal allowance of rain. And yesterday, we were sixty days from Sand Heads. It is a good passage for this season of the year in a deep ship. I think we shall just get home by Christmas.

The past two days, we have seen several vessels. Saturday night, I spoke a bark called the *Helen Mary*. Sunday, we were in company with a French bark about a mile or two distant. Today, nothing in sight except sundry albatrosses, Cape pigeons and other aquatic birds scaling about in search of a living. There are always albatrosses and Cape pigeons near the Cape.

I don't expect we shall see many more vessels until we get up to the equator. We may see some then. I do not intend to stop at St. Helena, although I have never passed before without stopping. But we are not in want of water or anything else. Therefore, it would be useless to stop and lose a day, besides some expense. Most vessels stop there to replenish their water. But we have had so much rain that

all our water barrels are full and we have as much fresh water aboard as when we left Sand Heads.

Last Saturday, the things of the sailor who died were sold at auction among the crew. They brought a great price for a sailor's effects. They sold high for a total of $107, which, with the $20 that was due him for wages, will be something to send his poor mother. You can usually learn something of a sailor from the amount his clothes sell for. If he is a poor, dissipated fellow, his chest is usually pretty light.

November 1 — Yesterday, at noon, we were directly opposite Cape Agulhas, the extreme south point of Africa, the doubling of which is called "rounding the Cape." It is not the Cape of Good Hope, itself. The Cape of Good Hope is farther north and west than Agulhas and it is out of the track of vessels unless bound for Cape Town. And, consequently, vessels do not see it. I have never seen the Cape of Good Hope, although I have been round it so often. Now, my love, we are steering a direct course for home. I told Mr. Fitzgerald that he might calculate to be in Boston by Christmas.

I did not intend to go in sight of St. Helena this time as it is a little off our course. But, as we have passengers on board who have never seen it, and no doubt would like to, I have changed my first intentions. It should be daytime when we pass the island. We'll run close in and show our signals and see what American vessels might be lying there.

November 6 — After dinner, my love, I read a little and, as I hardly knew what to do, I followed my daily practice and took a look at my dear little wife's miniature, kissed a lock of her hair which is neatly braided and enclosed in a paper with a lock of little Willie's. You know, dearest Sarah, that I think of you much oftener than I write, for you are the dearest treasure of my heart. I think of you and love you with my whole soul. Yes, my love, dearly, dearly do I love you. In less than two more months, I hope that I shall be comfortably seated at your side, chatting, and dancing our little boy upon my knee. The cold winter without will be forgotten in the warm happiness within.

We have had a fair wind and fair weather since we doubled the Cape and shall continue to have these for some weeks to come. It is here during this long spell of fine weather and fair winds that all returning Indiamen improve the opportunity to get their ship in good order. Everything about the rigging and sails, the hull and spars are cleaned and painted up so that the ship will make a decent appearance when going into port.

When "cleaning ship" on a homeward voyage, the sailors of the old square-riggers disliked the extra work, but they kept at it and always did a fine job. Nothing was ever overlooked. Commencing at the stern of the ship, the masts and yards were painted by a sailor who sat in a boatswain's chair and lowered himself at will as he worked. The rigging and backstays were "tarred down" and the decks were "holystoned." Down on their hands and knees, sailors with stones in their hands and sand on the decks rubbed from morning until night, day after day. With the tropical sun beating down on their backs and the deck sending up its scorching heat, it was punishing work, but it went on until every inch of the deck was holystoned. Then the sand was washed off and the deck was oiled. When all the work was done, the ship was spic and span, and ready for port.

November 12 — Yesterday at noon, our position placed the ship about thirty-three miles from St. Helena. As the wind grew lighter at about noon, I began to think that we could hardly reach the island before it grew too dark to see. And our passengers wanted to see it because it holds quite a place in history as the prison of Napoleon.

Noon came and no land in sight. One o'clock came with dinner on the table, and still no land to be seen. But I knew the island could be seen much farther off than we were unless it was enveloped in clouds. While at dinner, I told the passengers that by two o'clock when the sun had fallen a little more, I thought they could see it. When we came up from dinner, there was the island, directly ahead, looming up high, and partly covered with misty clouds,

which struck against its bold shores and enveloped it, shutting it almost from view.

Our breeze freshened and we rapidly drew near the island's sterile precipices. By four o'clock, we were up with the island. We passed around the east end of it, within a mile or a mile and a half of the shore. There was a bold, barren rock, towering one thousand five hundred or two thousand feet above our heads. The water was so deep that our ship could have run her bowsprit against the rocks and would not have touched the bottom.

In a little while more, we were up with the valley, at the mouth of which Jamestown is situated, this being the only town upon the island. It is where ships can lie. It is directly upon the lee side of the island and consists of houses built upon each side of the valley. There is a narrow road running directly from the sea. This zig-zags up the side of the valley. The mouth of the valley is somewhat wider than any other part and its whole front is lined with a heavy battery of guns. The place is fortified by a wall through which there is a gate by which you enter the town.

All over the island, in every accessible place, there are small batteries of guns. Every pinnacle has them. In addition to the island's fortifications by nature, all these make the island almost impregnable. It was all done when Napoleon was there. Now, there is only a small garrison, just to take care of the fortifications, as the death of Napoleon relieved the necessity of the island being so strictly guarded.

The neat little town looks very clean, huddled in between such great hills. There are rows of trees fronting the valley and you can hardly see a green thing elsewhere. Among the small cluster of houses rises quite a tall steeple of a church which, of course, looks small in contrast to the bold and rugged hills that surround it. But a church always adds to the beauty of any scenery where man has made a domicile. It looks cheerful and you seem to feel that you are amid civilization and near to people who recognize their Creator and Christ the Saviour and who strive to follow His teachings.

There are but few vessels lying in the little harbor. One is a Dutch ship that just came to anchor. There was also one large bark, a white ship that looked like an Ameri-

can whaler, but she showed no colors. There appeared to be several dismantled vessels lying there which I took to be slavers captured on the coast of Africa by the English squadron. At sunset, we were just past the island and all around looked pleasant. At ten o'clock, when we went to bed, the island's dark outline could just be perceived against the horizon by the bright, soft rays of a full moon.

November 16 — I intended to write a few lines yesterday, but the weather was unsettled and squally. Today, it is very bright and pleasant. Everyone about the ship is busy. The mates are getting the ship painted and the steward is cleaning the paint work in his cabin, getting ready to re-paint it.

This forenoon, the steward called me to look at a little stranger he found in a small room where he keeps flour barrels, upon the deck. And, lo, there was a toad squatted down upon his hind legs on the top of a flour barrel. Upon seeing that the steward was about to apply the broom to him, he retired from his elevated position with a long leap, and was soon out of sight. Of course, he had got on board at Calcutta, as you get all kinds of creatures on board ship in these tropical ports during the monsoon season. The other day, the mate caught a centipede in his berth and when we were in port at Calcutta, we killed two snakes on deck. They had got aboard in the hides.

Indeed, toads, rats, centipedes, and snakes were probably not the only creatures that were found aboard the *Delhi* during the return voyage from Calcutta, although they are the only ones that Captain Barry mentions. East Indiamen were famous for the insect life and vermin that were found on board during the homeward voyage from Calcutta. Various forms of pests came aboard with the jute and gunny cloth, and once there, they propagated with surprising rapidity. It has been said that " whoever left his boots outside his bunk at night found nothing in the morning but the nails and the eyelets." Another exaggerated statement declares that " an arrival from Calcutta in Boston was sometimes announced by a pack of terrified dogs running up

State Street pursued by an army of Calcutta cockroaches." Whatever the situation aboard the *Delhi* might have been in this respect, one can be pretty well assured that Captain Barry, out of respect for Sarah, did not reveal all of the facts in his journal.

November 20 — I told our passengers yesterday at noon that I thought it very probable that they would see the Island (Ilha) of Fernando de Noronha, which is a small island that belongs to Brazil and lies about two hundred miles off the extreme eastern point of South America. The island is about ten miles in length and quite picturesque. It is rugged granite or chalk, covered with small shrubbery, lichen and grass in most places, with here and there a thick growth of trees. The most remarkable feature of the island is a pyramid, or rock peak, which is elevated above the rest of the island. When you first see this peak, it appears like an immense church because there are hills so close to the peak that they look something like a roof.

While we were at dinner, the steward brought down his pastry and said that the land was in sight. Of course, after dinner, the passengers were all busy spying out the island. It has a garrison upon it and, near the peak, they had a flag flying. It looked quite pleasant there. But it must be a desolate place to live, for I suppose that vessels seldom stop there, unless occasionally there are some whalers coming from around Cape Horn. The steward said that a vessel he was once on stopped there one time. They got some water, poultry, pigs and vegetables, but these were exceedingly high priced.

November 25 — You will perceive from our position that we are once more in North Latitude and, of course, we begin to feel as though we are once more on our side of the house. At all events, my love, we are both of us now upon the same quarter of the globe, which we have not been for nearly a year.

We are now fairly into the northeast tradewinds and are making "straight wake" for home. Since I last wrote, I have shaved off my three month's beard and you may imagine that I am now beginning to look like myself again.

November 27 — We have seen today what we consider an old friend — or rather, an acquaintance on homeward voyages from India. I suppose you have heard sailors speak, or, perhaps, have read of a class of weed that floats over a large portion of the North Atlantic. Its proper name is " Facus Natans " but sailors generally call it " gulf weed." It is hardly ever seen south of 20 degrees North Latitude and seamen generally look for it, as it has a familiar appearance and seems, more fully than anything else, to make one realize that they are again in the North Atlantic and approaching their native land.

November 29 — I have a new order of a patient in the shape of insanity. It is one of my sailors. A day or two ago, the mate came to me and said he believed that the fellow was " cracked " as he acted rather strangely. I soon saw that his conduct confirmed this opinion. Of couse, as " physician general," I had to go to work and do for him. And now he is not so bad as he was, although on board a ship is not a very favorable place to doctor a person whose nervous system is affected. One of the men who had sailed with him before says that he was sun struck and crazy — lying in Madras Roads, and probably his present illness is some way connected with that.

　　To me, it is always a melancholy sight to see a person deprived of his reason, for then he has lost all — everything — future, friends and, indeed, every blessing which this life can afford, because he has fallen from the class of rational beings to a lower grade than the brute creation. For, although the brute has not reason, yet he has instinct such as he was born with, which serves his ends and desires. But a human being who has lost his reason is a mere machine which has lost its balance and regulation. It moves and does everything at random, without even the power to take care of itself. I hope my patient will get better, but I have not any great hopes, although he may.

　　We are now two thousand miles from home and we certainly ought to get there in three weeks more. I do hope to do it in less, if I can. I suppose it begins to look quite

winterish with you at home although here it is warm summer weather.

December 4 — Last Monday, we had quite an incident occur which got up a little excitement for a few minutes. About an hour after dinner, just as the people had returned to work, my crazy patient came on deck and made some remark to the steward who stood near the galley. The steward says to him to go below. A moment after, the fellow gave a leap and overboard he went. I was below and had just commenced folding up the leaves in my journal when I heard a hue and cry on deck. The first thing that occurred to me was that this fellow had got hold of a knife and was chasing someone about the deck.

I jumped up and asked what was the matter? A man overboard! Who was it? Robertson! We were going about six knots, with the studding sails set. The ship was immediately "rounded to" and the quarter boat cleared away. It was lowered down and pulled away for him.

The fellow struck out like a fish away from the boat. Before the boat got to him, he was nearly half a mile astern as the ship was going pretty fast through the water when he jumped overboard. We fished him up and in about half an hour, we were traveling again on our course. To prevent the fellow from doing himself or anyone else any harm, I had a pair of irons put upon his wrists and I kept him chained with a small chain. If I had a suitable place to confine him, I should not chain him. But, as I have not, I don't consider it safe for him to be at liberty. He might take it into his head to do some mischief.

It is not very pleasant to have the poor fellow in such a situation. But, there is no help for it and I doubt if the fellow will have his reason again. It was only last July, about a month before he came aboard to us, that he was sun struck.

December 6 — Yesterday was quite an unpleasant day. During the morning, we had the winds from almost all directions, from north to east-northeast, and then to the south where it remained fixed for the rest of the day, blowing a gale and, most of the time, with heavy rain and some thunder and lightning. The appearances were so threatening that I brought our ship under short sail.

The captains of the square-rigged ships prided themselves on their judgment as to how much sail their vessels could safely carry, and at what point during heavy weather it became unwise to continue to drive the ship. Captain Barry, like his contemporaries, liked to feel that he was taking full advantage of all the wind there was. Yet, at the same time, he was fully aware that any fool could "carry on," but only a wise man knew when to shorten sail in time. The real test of seamanship came with the approach of a storm when the capain had to decide how much he should shorten sail, and when. Good shipmaster that he was, Captain Barry was prudent enough to take the necessary precautions in time to avoid the risk of "running under" when driving before a storm. An incident on the ninth of December confirms this:

The morning looked pleasant today and it was quite moderate. A breeze sprang up and towards noon, it got to be quite a strong gale with a heavy sea on. We gathered in our canvas. The ship knocked about most famously. At dinner, it was hold on one moment and catch a mouthful the next, the passengers thinking that it required considerable dexterity to get even a mouthful.

As soon as I got through my dinner, I went upon deck, as it was bad weather. Soon, Mr. Cape came up, laughing. He said I did not stay to see the best of the fun. We had for our dinner a leg of boiled mutton and caper sauce, and a joint of roast mutton. It seems that in one of the heavy lurches by the ship, several of the smaller dishes as well as the large one containing the roast joint gave a jump off the table. The small dishes were saved by sliding into Mrs. Cape's lap but the joint shot clear of her and took further range by shooting into the open door of my stateroom. The steward scrambled away to secure the dishes and Mr. Fitzgerald secured the joint by tying a string to the knuckle and making it fast to the rack on the table.

About half an hour after this, we shipped a heavy sea which stove our quarter boat and started up the sail, started

off the bulwarks and smashed the carpenter's tool chest all
to pieces. Sundry persons were given a good wetting. I got
soaked from my head to my feet. But that is all part of a
sailor's life. After sunset, the gale moderated and by midnight, it was nearly calm.

December 12 — At noon today, we had soundings of fifty-two
fathoms and a muddy bottom. This is the first time that
our deep sea lead has been on Yankee ground for more than
a year.

Last night, there was a ship not a great distance from us
at sunset. About eleven o'clock this morning, this same ship
came quite near to us, asking for our longitude. We told
him what ours was and asked him his, which was nearly
three degrees different from ours. The ship proved to be
the *James Fagan* from Dublin and bound for New York
with steerage passengers. Finally, after some questions and
answers had passed, he said, " I wish you a pleasant voyage."
Of course, we thanked him, and wished him the same. At
the same moment, one of his worthy and respected passengers, right out of the bog, I suppose, sang out, " Jasus,
ye any baccy on board?" It was so unexpected that it set
every person upon our decks into broad laughter. I suppose
that "poor Pat" thought he had as good a right to hail us
as his captain had.

We had very unpleasant weather all day — wet, cold and
disagreeable. Just about noon, we saw a small English brig
not far from us, running down towards us with his colors
at half mast. So, we waited for him until he came up.
The wind was light and the sea smooth. Very soon we saw
that he had his boat out and pulling towards us.

The man in the boat came to see if we could spare him
some provisions. They wanted bread. I told him " yes " that
we could supply him, although not very good. We let him
have a couple of bags — about eighty or one hundred pounds
— and when he offered to pay for it, he had only a sovereign.
As that was rather more than the bread was worth and I
could not change it, having only a dime and a cent which
I had in my purse when I left America, I told him that
I would give him the bread.

The brig was called the *Dandy Jim* with a load of plaster

of paris bound for New York. He said they had been out twenty-eight days. His captain wanted to know my latitude and longitude, so I wrote it down on a piece of paper and gave it to the man who had come in the boat.

Before the days of good chronometers, a slight mistake in longitude when approaching Cape Cod meant running aground on Nantucket South Shoals. During dirty weather, sailing vessels from the West Indies, South America, and the Orient dared approach Boston only by the long detour of Vineyard Sound, Nantucket Sound, and the backside of Cape Cod. Returning East Indiamen were sometimes detained for weeks at Woods Hole or Vineyard Haven while awaiting good weather. And once they had rounded the Cape, sailing in Massachusetts Bay was danger-ous in bad weather. The irregular bottom gave a lead line no clue as to where the ship might be. When fog or snow obscured Boston Light, a mistake of a quarter of a point in the compass heading meant Cohasset rocks or The Graves. Captain Barry experienced his share of these common troubles:

December 15 — My patience is getting almost exhausted with continued head winds. Besides the head winds, there is the added discomfort of having both the air and the water only five or six degrees above the freezing point. We have had all last night and today a cold northeast and east wind. I think we could have possibly fetched up to Cape Cod, and probably from there into Boston, but it seems that this is not to be for the present because of the wind.

This morning, I tried to fetch the Shoals of Nantucket, but I got into shallow water and had to turn about. I know, my love, that you are beginning to expect me before this and are probably beginning to feel anxious. But you will know that the *Delhi* cannot be a great way off for I feel satisfied that the ship *James Fagan*, whom we spoke, has winds that would enable her to get to New York and she will report us. It seems strange that we seem to have the luck of getting poor chances in this dirty channel. It makes it rather hard work, working the ship, but when one gets into port and among his friends and finds them all well, he very soon forgets the disagreeable past.

December 16 — I must write my dear Sarah a few words to say that we are making our way with tolerable speed toward Cape Cod, and shall be up with it by eight o'clock this evening. But I do not expect to get much farther, for the weather is setting in so thick that we shall not make the light or land, and will be unable to run. I know by the looks of the weather that we will not have a very pleasant night, for the fog is so thick that one might almost cut it with a knife.

December 17 — Our breeze which we had yesterday, we could not take advantage of, after dark, owing to there being such a heavy, dense fog. I was up for the most part of the night, getting the ship along as far as I thought was prudent. About seven o'clock this morning, the fog cleared away with no wind and quite a calm. And there was Cape Cod, about four or five miles from us, to the southwest. Several vessels are about, in different directions and distances.

I do not see any prospect of arriving for a day or two, at least, although we are only four or five hours sail from Boston. You must not expect me to write very much, love, for I feel a little stupid as I only had one or two hours sleep, and I must lay down and get a nap. I may have to be up a good deal tonight if we should get a breeze.

December 21 — 4:00 A.M. — My own, dearest Sarah, I must write you one word with my cold fingers to say that we are passing Boston Light with a pilot aboard, and glad enough I am, for I have been since the fourteenth of this month in the South Channel with blowing thick weather, sometimes so I couldn't write or scarcely think of you. I have never had such a bad time there before. But now, love, I shall soon be with you, press you to this fond heart, kiss you and tell you how dearly I love you and our dear little boy.

The weather is looking bad and we have got in just in time, love. I shall write you from Boston as soon as possible. I cannot write more now, love. A kiss, another, and another.

Charles

Boston, December 22, 1847

My own dearest Sarah,

I cannot tell you how happy I feel being again in Boston and seated at a desk in the hotel, writing a letter to you, love. Your two letters I have received. You are all well, and I assure you that I was gratified enough to hear it. I am perfectly well and happy, and a few shades blacker than ever. I shall come home Saturday noon or night. I send you and Willie a thousand kisses with all the love in my heart. I must close and put this in the post that you may get it tomorrow. Good night, love and, believe me,

Your devoted and affectionate
Charles

IX

The Ship William Lord

The train bringing Captain Barry from Boston arrived at Kennebunk shortly after noon on Saturday, December 25, 1847. By only a scant few hours, he had won his four-month, fifteen-thousand-mile race with the calendar to be home by Christmas. The joy of his reunion with Sarah and little Willie is easy to picture.

The next two months were pleasant, indeed, for the happy couple and their little boy. Tired from his long voyage, Charles Barry relaxed and rested at the home of his father-in-law on Summer Street. But like many good things, the vacation ashore did not last very long. All too soon for Sarah and Charles, the *Delhi* was due to sail again. Early in February 1848, Captain Parrott notified Captain Barry that he was sending the ship out with another load of ice for Bombay and Calcutta. The vessel would be ready to sail by the middle of March.

Captain Barry had to leave Kennebunk on the first of March, as he was needed in Boston to supervise the loading of the *Delhi*. He also had to hire a crew and make the necessary preparations for sailing. Mr. Barnes would again be the mate. From the United States Hotel, Captain Barry wrote as follows to Sarah shortly after he arrived in the city:

> I did not find much detention of the "cars" on my trip
> up to Boston. I had Captain Parrott for company from

Portsmouth. We took seats together and chatted all the way up. Our ship is getting along as fast as can be but I am satisfied that we shall not get away until the second week this month.

This time, when Captain Barry sailed, Sarah took the train to Boston to see her husband off. Presumably, she left little Willie with her Aunt Mary or someone else in Kennebunk. Two weeks after he had departed on March 14, 1848, Captain Barry wrote the following in the journal which he again kept for Sarah:

It has been a fortnight today, dear Sarah, since you were aboard the *Delhi*. I shall receive a great deal of pleasure in associating my thoughts with that visit. There is one spot on the ship that will ever be sacred to me. It is where you jumped on the rail to see that vessel pass which had just arrived from the sea. I shall always look upon that spot as I walk upon the deck at twilight and think of you.

Much later during the voyage, Captain Barry wrote, " The *Delhi* seems to have all of her passages stereotyped. When you have seen the length of one, you may know what the length of the next will be between the same ports." And his second trip in the *Delhi* proved his point. Except for the time of year, his second voyage to India was almost identical with the first, although he did not have as many exciting adventures. The route was the same, the ship experienced almost the same high seas and periods of calm, and there was the usual amount of sickness among the crew.

There was, nevertheless, one notable difference between the two voyages, but it had nothing to do with sailing. It had to do with the presidential election in the United States. Since he had been inaugurated in March 1845, James K. Polk had been a controversial President, and Captain Barry had strong feelings about him. In fact, the captain heartily disapproved of Polk. Captain Barry was therefore exceedingly interested in the election of November 1848, but the *Delhi* departed from Calcutta on the twenty-third of December, before the news of the results of the American election had reached India.

Charles Barry was a staunch Whig. Besides the usual political differences that stemmed from party affiliation, the captain's dislike of the Democrat Polk was because he firmly believed that Polk's aggressive policies had caused the 1846 war with Mexico. There was some justification for Captain Barry's feelings.

Commencing when Texas had won its independence from Mexico in 1836, the slavery issue had brought the problem of the annexation of Texas into the open. Southerners and the slave-favoring Texans, themselves, wanted Texas annexed to the United States. President Martin Van Buren, who had held office from 1837 to 1841, had avoided the issue, because he was fearful of upsetting the balance of free and slave states. President Harrison, who succeeded him, did not live long enough in office to move one way or the other. But when John C. Calhoun became Secretary of State in 1844 under President John Tyler, of Virginia, who as Vice-President had taken office upon the death of Mr. Harrison, Calhoun worked out a treaty of annexation for the then Republic of Texas. The Senate failed to ratify the treaty, and the annexation of Texas therefore became the main issue of the 1844 presidential campaign. Because he favored it, James Polk won the election.

President Tyler accepted Polk's election as a mandate of the people and before Polk took office in March 1845, he rushed the annexation of Texas through Congress. Mexico immediately withdrew its representative from Washington. The southern boundary of Texas was in dispute, and shortly after his inauguration, Polk ordered " Old Rough and Ready" General Zachary Taylor to occupy the contested area. The Mexican War began in April 1846, with fighting in Texas and California. It ended in February 1848 with the Treaty of Guadalupe Hidalgo after a brilliant invasion of Mexico by " Old Fuss and Feathers " General Winfield Scott.

James Polk was an expansionist whose policies were opposed by Henry Clay, Daniel Webster, and John Calhoun. He approved the acquisition of California, Utah, and New Mexico as a part of America's "manifest destiny." He compromised on the Oregon boundary (" 54-40 or fight ") by accepting the 49th parrallel and giving Vancouver to the British. The Polk policies, in general, were adhered to by Lewis Cass, who became the Democratic candidate for President in 1848.

Cass was a former colonel in the regular army and a major general of volunteers. He had been Secretary of War under Andrew Jackson in 1831 and was a United States Senator from Michigan at the time of his nomination for President. At the Whig convention that year, Zachary Taylor defeated Winfield Scott as the Whig candidate for President. During the presidential election in November, the anti-slavery Democrats defected from their party by voting for the free-soil candidate, former President Martin Van Buren. As a result, Lewis Cass lost the election to Zachary Taylor. But Captain Charles Barry, who was in Indian waters with the *Delhi* at the time, had no way of knowing this.

The captain was at sea, homeward bound from Calcutta, on the 1849 Inauguration Day in the United States. His journal entry for that day expresses his sentiments about the matter in no uncertain terms:

Sunday, March 4 — Today we are a thousand miles nearer to each other, my love, than we were last Sunday, and on this memorable fourth of March, we are entered upon west longitude, which makes it seem as though we are again in the same half of the globe.

I call this fourth of March memorable because it ushers in the day on which Mr. Polk of warlike notoriety ceases to be President of the United States. And I wish upon his retiring from the office he has so unworthily filled that he could say to himself that " I leave the presidential chair, and in leaving it, I leave no more stain upon the character of my country than the blot that the name James K. Polk makes, when written, upon the pages of my country's history." But, I fear, he cannot conscientiously say that, and if he thinks he can, I feel equally sure that no good man can say as much for him.

I suppose that either General Cass or General Taylor has been elected to the office of President. Their chances,

I think at this distance from home, are about equal. But if there is any difference, it would be in favor of General Taylor and I hope, of the two, that he has been chosen for I consider Cass as one of the most dangerous men that could be elected to the presidency.

Ten days later, Captain Barry again mentioned the new President in his journal:

Thursday, March 15 — In a couple of days, now, we shall be in the track of outward bound vessels on their way to India, South America, and so forth. Mayhap, we shall have the chance to speak some ship not long from home. I should like to know who is President.

Finally, a whole month after the new President had been inaugurated, the captain solved the mystery:

Friday, April 6 — We ought to begin to see some vessels soon as we are in the track of vessels bound from the United States to the West Indies. It always seems as if we were drawing nearer home when we can fall in with a " Johnathon " bound out to the West Indies with a load of lumber.

Later — My dear, we have just learned a piece of news and I have taken out my journal to tell it to you, although, of course, it is no news to you.

I had just put away my pen and paper when the mate sang out at the skylight to the cabin that there was a schooner running down towards us and that it would come pretty near. I went up on deck and had the colors hoisted. As our vessels neared each other, we saw that he had American colors. We hauled up our mainsail and, when he got near enough, we hailed him. It was the schooner *Craven* from Philadelphia. " Who is President?" I called. He understood and replied " General Taylor."

I swung my trumpet [i.e., megaphone] around my head and gave a cheer, for we had thought among us that the election might have been somewhat uncertain and that we might have heard that it had been General Cass. And I think that he would be a very poor man to be President. The wind was blowing so fresh that we were soon past the other vessel.

In due course, the *Delhi* rounded Cape Cod, thirteen months after she had departed from Boston. For once, Captain Barry experienced good weather for his arrival at his home port. The final entry in his journal for Sarah tells the homecoming story:

Monday Morning, April 30 — Home, home again, my dearest Sarah, and soon I shall hear from you. Yesterday at sunset, we had a fine, pleasant breeze spring up from the north, with a bright and pleasant starlit night. We ran along at a fine rate. At about eleven o'clock, we passed a large fleet of vessels bound out, and at midnight, there was Boston Light, all in sight. I can assure you that it was a pleasant sight to me after such a long absence from home, with the prospect of soon being in the society of my dear wife and child, together with our friends.

    As we drew up towards the light, our fine breeze began to die away. We tried to get a pilot by showing a blue light and occasionally throwing up a rocket. But we did not succeed until daylight, when we saw a boat come poking out from behind the lighthouse. They had been comfortably sleeping all night. We got the pilot aboard just after sunrise which, of course, relieved me from the charge of the ship. We had soon got out of him all the news that he could furnish us. You may rest assured, my dearest Sarah, that I, for one, felt happy enough to find myself going up Boston Harbor.

    About ten o'clock, we came to anchor, and I soon packed myself away in a boat to go on shore and hear the news from home, sweet home. May our kind and Heavenly Father be praised for all his goodness toward us and that He has continued us in health and prosperity, and preserved us from harm and danger, and brought us again together after so long and so distant a separation.

    — Finished at Boston, April 30, 1849

Captain Barry felt that the year-long voyages to India were too much for a family man. Before leaving Boston the first week in May to return home to Kennebunk, he terminated his business relations with Captain Parrott and resigned command of the *Delhi*. From now on, he had decided, he would only sail on shorter voyages.

With her husband away, it had been a long, difficult year for Sarah. Not only had it been necessary for her to care for her own son, William, but she also had been helping with the younger Lord children, especially with her little sister Mary, who was then only four and a half years old. It was a joyous day, indeed, when Charles came back to Kennebunk to bring an end to many, many months of anxiety.

The 1840 decade had been a prosperous one for the maritime industries upon which the coast of Maine depended for its livelihood. The investments and various business enterprises of Sarah's father had done very well during this period and he had commenced to prosper more than ever before. He was now the sole owner of three vessels and was having a fourth built at Kennebunk Landing. Upon the return of his son-in-law from India, he bought a house next to the Second Congregational Church on Dane Street in Kennebunk Village, which he rented to Charles and Sarah at a very reasonable rate. For the first time, in the early summer of 1849, the happy couple and their son were able to move into a home of their own.

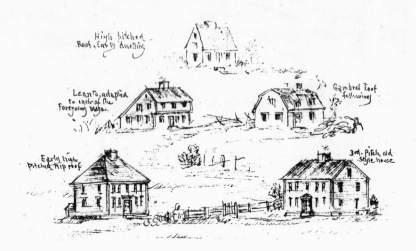

High pitched Roof, Early dwelling

Leanto, adapted to each of the foregoing bldgs.

Gambrel Roof following

Early, high pitched Hip roof

3rd. Pitch, old style house

SHIP *MT. WASHINGTON*

From a painting made in December 1847. Tonnage: 547.29. Hail: Kennebunk, Maine. Master and principal owner: Jotham Blaisdell. Builder: Asa M. Durrell, Kennebunk Landing. Captain Charles Barry also owned an interest in this ship. Although he never sailed her, the vessel was typical of the other cotton carrying ships of her day, and very similar to, though smaller than, the ship *William Lord,* of which Captain Barry was master.

All of William Lord's vessels had been Kennebunk-built. The first was the brig *Swiss Boy,* which had been launched at the yard of George W. Bourne in December 1837. This was followed by the ship *Hartley* (469 tons) in October 1845 and the bark *Francis Watts* (255 tons) in August 1846. Early in 1849, he ordered his largest ship to that date, the 743-ton *William Lord,* which he had named after himself. The ship was to be built by Clement Littlefield, who was one of those who had his ship-yard at Kennebunk Landing. The vessel was designed for the cotton carrying trade between American southern ports and England.

Principally for Sarah's sake, Mr. Lord was pleased with Captain Barry's decision to make no more India voyages. Partly to encourage Charles to sail only on shorter trips and partly because Charles was known to be one of the best shipmasters in the business, Lord offered him the command of his new ship. The offer was quickly accepted.

Charles Barry had commenced to save and invest some of the money he had been earning. Not only did he agree to command the *William Lord,* but he also bought an interest in the ship from his father-in-law. The vessel became the second in which he now owned a part. The year before, the captain had purchased a financial interest in the Kennebunk ship *Mt. Washington.* This was a vessel of 547 tons that had been built during 1847 in the yard of Asa M. Durrell at Kennebunk Landing. The *Mt. Washington's* principal owner was Captain Jotham Blaisdell, who was also the ship's master.

As he had done while the *Oakland* was being built by Henry Kingsbury, Captain Barry spent a great deal of time during the late summer and fall of 1849 at Kennebunk Landing. He made himself thoroughly familiar with every detail of the new ship. Though larger, it was quite similar to both the *Oakland* and the *Mt. Washington,* which was natural as all three were full-rigged ships designed primarily for the cotton carrying trade.

That a ship as large as the *William Lord* could be built at Kennebunk Landing had been made possible in 1848 by the construction of a lock at a point known as the Narrows on the

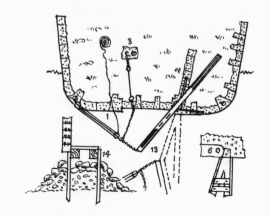

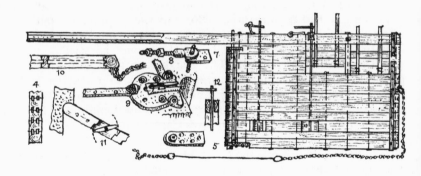

The Lock.

Kennebunk River below the Landing. The lock was designed to retain and regulate, when necessary, the fresh water that flowed down the river, as well as the tidewater that flowed up the river when the tide was coming in. The lock made it possible to launch much bigger ships at the Landing. The vessels were floated down the river as far as the Narrows, where they waited for high tide. Then the lock was opened to permit them to be warped the rest of the way down to Kennebunkport.

The massive gates for the lock, fourteen feet, eight inches by twenty-three feet, five inches, had been built in the yard of Bourne and Kingsbury. These had heavy beams extending twenty-seven feet, six inches out from their hinged end to aid in their opening and closing, as well as to balance the weight of the gate. The entire project, which had cost fifty-five hundred dollars, had been financed by the sale of stock.

The ship *William Lord* was launched on November 1, 1849. The vessel was then warped downstream, through the lock, to Kennebunkport. Here, her masts were stepped, the rudder hung, the rigging installed, and the sails fitted. These had been made in the sail loft of John Manning at Kennebunkport.

The *William Lord* made her maiden voyage during the last week in November, when Captain Barry sailed the ship to Boston. His first mate was a Kennebunk man named William Ross. Having no cargo, the ship sailed in ballast, this consisting of rocks that had been gathered from the surrounding countryside at Kennebunkport. At Boston, Captain Barry added more men to his crew, then proceeded in ballast to New York where he loaded a mixed cargo of manufactured goods and imported European products that he carried to Philadelphia. Here he spent Christmas 1849 while waiting for a cargo he could take to one of the southern ports. Which port this might be did not make much difference, as the *William Lord* could obtain cotton to carry to Liverpool at almost any of the larger coastal cities from Charleston, South Carolina, to New Orleans.

Before leaving Kennebunk, Captain Barry had known that Sarah was going to have another baby about the end of February. When the expected time arrived, he was at Mobile, Alabama, loading cotton for England. Early in March, a letter arrived just before he sailed. It was from his father-in-law and had been addressed in care of the office of Herbert C. Peabody, the Mobile cotton broker through whom the ship's cargo had been purchased. Much to Captain Barry's relief, the letter conveyed the happy tidings that Sarah's baby had been born at the Barry home on Dane Street on February 28, 1850. "The event took place during the night," wrote Mr. Lord. "Sarah continues very comfortable and is getting along very well. The babe is well and is a fine boy. They all say he is very handsome. Sarah has a very good nurse."

Captain Barry did not see his new son until he returned to Boston from Liverpool at the end of April. With but little time to spare before he was due to sail again, he made a hurried trip to Kennebunk. He and Sarah named the child Charles Dummer Barry, the middle name being the surname of Sarah's uncle by marriage, who lived in Washington. But Charles could not stay around very long to enjoy his new son. The first of May, he had to sail from Boston once more to take the *William Lord* to New Orleans.

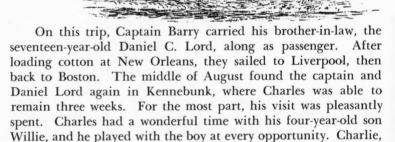

On this trip, Captain Barry carried his brother-in-law, the seventeen-year-old Daniel C. Lord, along as passenger. After loading cotton at New Orleans, they sailed to Liverpool, then back to Boston. The middle of August found the captain and Daniel Lord again in Kennebunk, where Charles was able to remain three weeks. For the most part, his visit was pleasantly spent. Charles had a wonderful time with his four-year-old son Willie, and he played with the boy at every opportunity. Charlie, the baby, was still too small to be fully appreciated by his father.

Even so, Captain Barry rather clumsily did what he could to help Sarah care for the child. And when they were not busy with the children, Sarah and Charles visited with their many friends or entertained both friends and members of Sarah's large family at the house on Dane Street.

But in spite of their love for each other and the happiness they both derived from their marriage, matters during this three-week period were not always blissfully tranquil at the Barry home. Charles had married relatively late in life and was understandably quite decided in his likes and dislikes. In some ways, this man who had spent many years alone at sea as the absolute master of his ocean-going domain was a bit fastidious in his preferences. Sarah, on the other hand, was used to the unsystematic routine of a large family where everyone usually did just about as he pleased, and when he pleased. Nevertheless, she tried her best to run her house as her husband wanted, even though this must have been difficult at times. Though they had now been married for five years, Charles had been away at sea so much of the time that, in some ways, the couple had hardly had time to become adjusted to each other.

Just what happened between Charles and Sarah during Charles's vacation in Kennebunk is open to speculation. From one of Captain Barry's letters later, it is evident that Sarah at one time begged him not to go to sea again. But this, apparently, was a request he could not, or would not, grant at the time, probably because he felt that he had not yet saved enough money to be able to remain ashore. What may have caused even more emotional distress than this between the captain and his wife can be readily surmised from the following extract from a letter that Charles wrote to Sarah after he had left Kennebunk:

> If I could only be at home, I think we would be as happy as a snug little family could be. We should then be rid of these long separations and become, all of us, assimilated to each other. You would be free from so many cares and troubles, for I would put them upon my own shoulders

and you would not have to bear them all. Yes, dearest,
I would do all I could to make everything at home very
happy. It would be my aim to accomplish that. It almost
brought the tears, my love, to see you give way to imaginary
dreams about the time that will come when I shall care
nothing about you and do not love you, or that you do not
suit me, and so forth. It makes me feel unpleasant to have
you indulge in any such thoughts, even though they have no
foundation in reality. I know they cause you to feel unhappy. You should not give way to thoughts which have
no reality, for I do love you, my dear Sarah, more than you
can imagine. If you could, you would not indulge in such
reveries.

I would not be without you for all the world. Besides,
it is you, dearest, who makes my home the one spot on earth
that is the most pleasant for me to rest my thoughts. You
must not think, dear Sarah, that you do not suit me, or
that I am too particular, for I assure you that I am far
from feeling any dissatisfaction. I do not intend to be
particular, for I can accommodate myself to any kind of
living. Could I be at home long enough at a time, we
would soon fall into each other's ways. Were I at home
permanently, I should accommodate myself to your ways, in
this respect. But I am away so much that my habits of living are formed differently, that I cannot change them all at
once, in the course of two or three weeks. The next time
I come home, I may, perhaps, stay longer and I shall be
very careful not to say or do anything which may hurt your
feelings.

And you, my dear Sarah, must endeavor not to be too
sensitive, for those who have too thin a skin are apt to get
smarted, continually. I reckon, my dear, that you need not
give yourself any uneasiness about your cooking, for I shall
be perfectly satisfied with what you are satisfied with. When
you hear that I am coming home again, you must not build
any air castles, without any foundation, that you won't be
able to suit Charles, and work yourself into a fever of un-
happiness without any cause. If you do, you will spoil your
pretty face, love, and, besides, you will be less capable of
conferring happiness upon those whose happiness you wish
to promote. Now, my dear, we will dismiss all these imagi-

nary troubles about an inability to confer happiness upon each other. I will promise to do as you wish and I will take care of myself and health when away. And you will do the best you can at home while we are compelled to be so much separated. I will consent that you may box my ears, and kiss me, too, at any time you wish.

The *William Lord* was due to depart from Boston on the tenth of September — which meant Captain Barry's vacation in Kennebunk was terminated on the sixth. The ship was to sail in ballast to New York, where she would pick up cargo for Baltimore. From Baltimore, Captain Barry and his father-in-law had decided that the vessel should be taken to one of the southern ports where cotton for Liverpool could be purchased in the open market. Savannah, the men had concluded, was the most likely place to try to buy cotton at that particular time.

When Captain Barry bid farewell to Sarah early in September, he was more reluctant than ever to leave home. His parting from the family he loved so well appears to have been sadder than usual. The tiff that he and Sarah had had probably weighed heavily upon his mind, and it is not impossible that he may have had some sort of a premonition of what the next few months might have in store for him. On September 17, he wrote Sarah from New York, saying, in part:

It seems an age, dearest, since I left you and I can assure you that I left home with a heavy, heavy heart. While seated in the cars going up to Boston, I found my thoughts continually resting upon home, dear home, my eyes filling with unbidden tears. I felt aware that every moment was increasing the distance which separated us. I have felt somewhat homesick, but this is a feeling that it will not do for a sailor to give way to, and I must make the best of what I cannot avoid.

I shall endeavor to leave Baltimore this week and if you write me there, direct your letter care of Spregklenson and Weir. Should either of the children be taken sick with the summer complaint, I would send for the doctor in good season. . . . .

CAPTAIN CHARLES EDWARD BARRY
From a painting by an unknown artist

X

Mutiny

Captain Barry reached the mouth of the Savannah River on October 4, 1850. Knowing that it might take quite some time to obtain a cargo of cotton, he anchored the *William Lord* at an anchorage known as Tybee Roads, near the mouth of the river, approximately fifteen miles below the City of Savannah. He used the ship's quarter boat to go ashore at Savannah Beach where he engaged a carriage to take him up to the city. The mate, William Ross, remained aboard ship in charge of the vessel and the crew. On the sixth of October the captain wrote a letter to Sarah in which he described some of the troubles he was commencing to encounter:

I hardly need to tell you how happy I felt yesterday morning at receiving your long letter of September 30th. The ship is still below the city and I am boarding at the Pulaski House. I have to pay pretty high board and the house is poor enough, too, for the best hotel in the place. I long to have the ship up so that I can have a home of my own and live aboard comfortably.

Unwittingly, Captain Barry had arrived at Savannah to buy and load cotton at an inopportune time. Speculators had rigged the market for cotton and there was none to be had at a reasonable price. But optimistically the captain hoped that the market would break at almost any moment. His letter to Sarah continued:

I think I shall bring the ship up sometime this week, as I have fully concluded to remain here and try my chances [i.e., wait at Savannah for better prices rather than sail on to another southern port to try to buy cotton]. I think I shall manage to do something ere a great while.

I expect that I and anyone at this house will eat their full allowance of dirt that a sailor is said to have to eat before he dies — that is, a peck. When I went to my room, I opened the table drawer to put in a couple of letters and found that the drawer was half full of cockroaches. I went to the washstand to wash and took off the towel which was lying over the top of the pitcher. The pitcher and the water were both covered with ants. At the supper table, I cut a corn cake and at the same time, divided a part of an egg shell that was inside of it. I thought to myself that I should not like to peep into the kitchen and have an insight into its mysteries. Drops of water from many a dark brow no doubt help out the gusto of some of the food we have to eat.

This morning after I had taken my wash, I threw the towel, soaking wet, under the table. Just now, when I came up to write, I found the blackened towel on the back of a chair to dry, in readiness to wipe my face the next time I have occasion to do so. I intend to send for the ebony lady who has care of the rooms and give her a bit of a scolding. I took care to put the towel in the sand box which is in the room to serve as a spittoon. From this you can judge how well the best hotel in the place is kept. They are building a new hotel of better and larger description and I am sure that there is want enough for it. I shall not feel right until I get my ship up so I can live on board. Then, love, I shall spend a good many of my idle moments writing to you.

The weather here is pleasant, cool and clear. But I should think that about half of the population were, or had been, sick with the fever. You never saw such a lot of sick looking faces walking about on the streets, and everyone you hear asks another how he does. "Well, I'm getting about," is the reply. So many of the laboring men are laid up with the fever that they are quite scarce.

You must give my love to Willie, dearest, and tell him that his father inquires about him. Tell him that I shall write him a letter before long if he behaves and is a good boy. As for Charlie, I can only send the little fellow a kiss and he will not know where it came from.

I don't know how soon I can write you again, love. Perhaps not for a week. It will depend some on how I am situated. I hope to bring the ship up some time this week, and then I shall feel at home and be more conveniently situated for writing.

About ten days after the *William Lord* had arrived at the mouth of the Savannah River, Captain Barry brought the ship upriver to Savannah. He tied up at a wharf on the waterfront along the Marsh Island Channel, opposite Hutchinson Island. Then he moved his living quarters from his room at the Pulaski House to his cabin aboard the vessel. It wasn't customary, but he did it anyway. "I suppose that I should sleep on shore until the frost comes, even after the ship comes up," he had written Sarah, adding: "All the captains in summer sleep on shore, as it is not considered healthy to sleep on board until the frost has killed the vegetation."

The price of cotton did not drop in the manner Captain Barry had hoped. A week after he had brought the ship upriver, he discharged the vessel's crew, retaining only the ship's officers, the steward, and the colored cook. It was not until mid-November, six weeks after arriving at the mouth of the Savannah River, that he was able to close a deal for a cargo of cotton at a price that assured a profit for the voyage to England.

When the time came, the captain experienced great difficulty in obtaining men for a new crew. In the end, he had to journey to Charleston, South Carolina, where the only men he could find were a motley collection of seafaring ruffians to whom he had to give an advance on their wages before they would sign up for the Liverpool voyage.

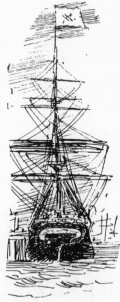

The ship was loaded at Savannah by stevedores who had all of the cargo aboard by the first of December. But it was almost a week after that before Captain Barry was able to get the ship downriver to Tybee Roads. On the sixth, he wrote to Sarah as follows:

My dearest Sarah,
    I must improve the opportunity to commence another letter to my heart's dearest treasure. I came down the river this noon with six men I had hired for $18 to bend the ship's sails and get her in readiness for sea while we are waiting to get our crew over from Charleston. I am obliged to go up to town again to finish my business and clear the ship at the Custom's House. When I go up, I shall stop at the Pulaski House, even if I do have to pay $2 a day for a dirty room.

This was to be the captain's last voyage for quite a while. He owned an interest in the *William Lord*'s cargo from which he hoped to make a good profit. Further on in this letter he mentioned it:

    If I should succeed in getting a good return freight from Liverpool, I shall make enough money to pay one year's family expenses. I ought to be able to stop at home one year upon our return. I wish that business will become a little better by then so that the *Mt. Washington* will be earning some money, even if I am not earning any myself. I will take the chance of getting a fresh start again for the sea. I shall not find it difficult to obtain a ship when I want one, either out of Kennebunk or out of Boston.
    I suppose that by this time of the day you have disposed of your cares, Master Willie and Master Charlie, and have put them to bed, side by side, where they are snoozing away. Willie always looks so free and easy when a-bed and asleep with his arms tossed about in any direction. — One more kiss, love, and good night.
Charles

More than a week went by and Captain Barry still didn't sail because he had no crew. The men he had hired and given advance wages at Charleston did not report for duty. When he had gone up to Savannah to clear his business there, the captain had enlisted the help of the sheriff. In the interim, the

fever that was everywhere around had commenced to catch up with the captain himself. Back on board the *William Lord,* he wrote to Sarah on Sunday, December 15:

My dear Sarah,

As I have a few moments, I will write a few lines and have them ready to send by the pilot if we should succeed in getting the ship to sea. I am in a good deal of trouble with my sailors who are in a state of mutiny and are a great annoyance to me. I have so many things to occupy my thoughts, time and attention that I have had hardly any time to think of you, dearest, and our little ones. And, with all my troubles, I have to give a thought or two to my own ailments as I do not find my health just what I would wish it to be.

After I last wrote you, dear Sarah, I had to send in pursuit of my men who were to come from Charleston. After two days tramping about sixty miles from Savannah, the sheriff succeeded in taking all but one of them. I hired boats and men to watch and take them down the river and put them on board my ship. I then cleared at the Customs House and followed down myself in another boat. After paying $140 for catching the men, they went to work on board. But the next morning, eight out of thirteen refused to do duty. They weren't going to sea in the ship unless they went in irons. They would do nothing in their villainy except cheat the ship out of their advance wages.

Some of them, I have put in irons one place, and some I have shut up in other places. I endeavor to keep them separated all I can. With my mates, I have to keep a night watch, and work in the bargain. We have just enough men to manage to get the anchor up, with all there are on board to work. I hope soon to get a moderate wind so that we can drift out to sea. Then I will try, when I need their services to raise the sails, to make my prisoners work. They will work or starve.

These are the villains for whom people build sailor's homes and give so much in sympathy, when they might just as well throw oil upon a fire, for all the good it does. Nothing will ever benefit or reform sailors, except to do away entirely with paying them advance wages before the wages have been earned. And while I think of it, Sarah, I wish you immediately to have your name withdrawn from the membership and as a contributor to the Sailor's Home. Give your charity in any other way you please, but not to hardened villains. The money which I obtain by following the sea is too hard earned to contribute even one mill upon such unworthy objects.

I have never in my life had quite so much trouble in getting out of port. Think what this detention and expense means to the owners of this ship and cargo, all because of the misconduct of these wretches, to say nothing of the disagreeable necessity of the officers to have to go to sea with only six men on duty and all the rest in a state of mutiny. I told these sailors that, as sure as there was a God in Heaven, they were going to sea in this ship. And if they find me to relinquish what I set out for, when I am right, they will find me different from what I think myself to be.

It causes me to work and have a great deal of anxiety and care to go to sea in winter with a crew in such a state. But I care nothing for that if my health will only hold out sufficiently, so I can be a man, myself.

I would love to see our dear little boys, Sarah. There is Willie with his red, glowing cheeks and full of life, wishing it were not Sunday, so he could draw his sled about. And little Charlie, I suppose, makes his way up to the fire in the grate at every opportunity, giving his mother all the trouble he can, to watch him. Dear home, sweet home is such a paradise of a place compared to being surrounded by a lot of hardened, reckless sailors. Now I will bring my letter to a close, dear Sarah, as we may be able to get to sea on this afternoon tide. — One more kiss, love.

Your affectionate Charles

Monday, December 16 — Dearest, we did not get to sea yesterday, so I shall add one line to my letter. I shall not write much for I do not feel very well. I have some pain and a few days before I left town, I lost my appetite. I reduced my weight in three days from 126 down to 121 pounds.

I have much internal distress and nothing that I have taken has helped the trouble I am having with my liver. Perhaps you will think that all the delays and troubles I have had are because I am going to sea against my wife's wishes. Perhaps this is so, for everything has gone against me so far this trip. Four of my refractory sailors have gone to their work and now I have only three of them in confinement. Just now, as I am writing, another has wanted to come out and go to work. I have let him do so. I reckon they will all get sick of leisure before long.

We have a wind blowing now that will take us out to sea if it is not too thick outside to see our way out. I think our prospect of getting to sea this afternoon is so good that I shall fold my letter and get it ready to send by the pilot, for he will soon be wishing to get the ship underway.

I must have one more kiss, my love, even if it is upon this paper. I will place one, just here, for you. Kiss our little boys for me. How dearly I should like to be home and see the little fellows. My remembrance to all at home.
                    — Your devoted, affectionate Charles.

This final letter to Sarah, which had been written on December 15 and 16, 1850, then given to the pilot who mailed it in Savannah, was the last that was ever heard directly from Captain Charles Edward Barry, who would have been forty years old in January. The ship *William Lord* never reached Liverpool. She was due there not later than the latter part of January 1851, and news of her safe arrival was expected at Kennebunk by the first or second week in February. Yet no news came. One can easily visualize the distraught Sarah Barry scanning the MARINE JOURNAL in the *Portland Transcript,* searching hopefully under the "Arrivals" and "Spoken" column, then fearfully looking in the black box headed "Disasters." But nothing at all was ever again heard from the ship or from any of the men she carried.

After nearly all hope had passed, Sarah's father wrote a letter to a friend — a steamship captain who had also sailed from Savannah to England at about the same time that Captain

Barry was preparing to depart from the mouth of the Savannah River in the *William Lord*. In due course, the following reply was received:

New York
April 6, 1851

Mr. William Lord
Kennebunk, Maine

Dear Sir:
Your favour of the 31st instant is received, requesting me to give you what information I can respecting Captain Barry whom I am sorry to learn is much out of time, but trust that he is yet safe and will be restored to his family.

On the 15th of December, in going down the Savannah River with steam, I passed and spoke with Captain Barry. He then appeared well and all right on board, although he had had some difficulty with his crew. On the 16th, I left the river about 4:00 P.M. At that time, the *William Lord* was about four miles astern, under way, and I supposed that he went to sea that night, until I arrived at Liverpool where I learned that he did not leave the river until the 21st, for what reason I did not learn. Our passage out was a rough one, but perhaps not more so than might be expected at that season of the year. His ship was in good trim for a cotton loaded one. When I parted with Captain Barry at Savannah, he appeared in good spirits, as he had been during his stay in Savannah.

I am sorry, sir, that I cannot give you any more encouraging information.

Yours very respectfully,
/s/ James Borland

One can only speculate upon what might have happened aboard the sturdy, square-rigged *William Lord*. What could have caused Captain Barry to have remained in the vicinity of the mouth of the Savannah River for five days after the pilot had been dropped? Could his illness have become worse, to the extent that he could not command the ship? And if so, why did not the mate, William Ross, bring the ship back to port?

Or did the mutinous crew manage to overpower Captain Barry and his officers in an attempt to steal the ship, only to lose her at sea because they were unable to sail her? It is entirely possible that the captain and the officers might even have been killed by the mutineers. Or did the ship finally depart from Savannah under near normal circumstances, only to later founder at sea in a storm? No one will ever know.

SARAH CLEAVES BARRY
From a daguerreotype presumed to have been made sometime between 1850 and 1860

Epilogue

The loss of Captain Barry, his first officer, William Ross, and the ship *William Lord* was but one part of a double tragedy to descend upon the people of Kennebunk. A second Kennebunk ship, which had been built in the same yard and bore the same family name as the *William Lord,* sailed from Liverpool for the United States on the same day that Captain Barry was reported to have left Savannah for England — December 21, 1850. By a singular coincidence, this ship, too, was never heard from again. She was the 546-ton *Susan Lord,* owned by Samuel H. Gould and commanded by Captain F. W. Chadbourne. The ship had been launched at Kennebunk Landing by Clement Littlefield on September 6, 1847.

The widowed Sarah Barry with her two young sons continued to live in the house on Dane Street. Several years after Captain Barry had been declared legally dead, she married a retired sea captain, shipowner, and trader named Jott Stone Perkins. Jott Perkins, a bachelor, was one of four brothers who carried on the business their father had started for trading with the West Indies under the firm name of Eliphalet Perkins and Sons. Jott Perkins bought the house on Dane Street from William Lord, then later, he purchased the house next to the William Lord home on Summer Street. Here, he and Sarah lived happily and raised the two Barry children.

William Edward Barry (1846-1932), whom Sarah and Charles had called "Little Willie," always lived in Kennebunk. In adult life, he practiced architecture and became locally noted as a historian and naturalist. The youngest Barry son, Charles Dum-

WILLIAM LORD'S BRICK STORE ON MAIN STREET, KENNEBUNK

As it appeared during the 1880 period or earlier. This building — the one in the center with two chimneys — was built by William Lord in 1825 and today is the home of the nationally known Brick Store Museum.

Photo courtesy The Brick Store Museum

mer Barry (1850-1921), became a successful business man, and before he retired, was the senior partner of the mercantile shipping firm of Henry W. Peabody and Company, with offices in New York, Boston, and several foreign ports.

The brick store across Main Street from the First Congregational Church of Kennebunk, which was built and owned by William Lord, remained the property of his direct descendants for one hundred and twenty-two years. On June 11, 1947, the building was presented to The Brick Store Museum, which had been incorporated seven years earlier. Today, the building is open to the public and serves as the repository for data and objects of local historical interest and value, especially those pertaining to the old shipbuilding and seafaring days for which Kennebunk was famous.

Full-rigged Ship.

1. Flying jib.
2. Outer jib.
3. Inner jib.
4. Fore topmast staysail.
5. Fore-course or foresail.
6. Lower fore topsail.
7. Upper fore topsail.
8. Lower fore topgallant sail.
9. Upper fore topgallant sail.
10. Fore royal.
11. Main course or mainsail.
12. Lower main topsail.
13. Upper main topsail.
14. Lower main topgallant sail.
15. Upper main topgallant sail.
16. Main royal.
17. Cross-jack (pr. cro'jack).
18. Lower mizzen topsail.
19. Upper mizzen topsail.
20. Lower mizzen topgallant sail.
21. Upper mizzen topgallant sail.
22. Mizzen royal.
23. Driver or spanker.

GLOSSARY

This glossary is not an attempt to define all of the nautical words and terms in the vernacular of the sailors who manned square-rigged ships. To the contrary, it only explains the words and phrases in the text of this book that may not be familiar to readers who are not entirely conversant with the language of the sea.

It might be well at the outset to note that a sailor never *ties* a knot, for a knot is always *made* or *put in*. A hitch in a line or rope aboard ship is always *taken* or *made fast*. A sailor *puts in* a splice, *bends* two ropes together and *works* a fancy knot such as a Turk's Head or a sennit. He *clamps on* a seizing and *clears* a tangled rope by *overhauling* it. Rope is always coiled *down*, never up, and when the coil must be turned over, a sailor *capsizes* it. A ship is *secured* for the sea by *lashing down* everything on deck which is movable, and a sailor *freshens the nip* of a sheet or halyard by taking-up or slackening it to bring the wear or chafing to a different place. A *hitch* is used to make a rope fast to another object, while a *bend* secures the ends of two ropes to each other. A *lashing* secures one object to another object with rope or *small stuff*, which is the name used for string or light cord. A *seizing* binds ropes together or to other objects, more or less permanently. A *stopping* serves in much the same manner, though temporarily, while a *whipping* is a binding of sail-twine or *marline*, marline being a small line made up of two strands held together by a loose, left-hand twist.

In their everyday talk, the men who dealt with square-rigged sailing ships spoke with such words as these:

About (to come *about*) — for a ship under sail to take a different direction, as in tacking, when a ship is beating (sailing) to windward (towards the wind) and changes her course by allowing the wind to exert its pressure on the other side of the sails.

Adze — A cutting tool with a handle like an axe, though different from an axe because the arching blade is set at right angles to the handle. Adzes are used to make a log into a timber and to smooth, or trim, the rough surfaces of planks.

Aft — In, at, or near the stern of a ship.

Aloft — In, or into, the top of the masthead (top of the mast), or the higher yards, or rigging above the ship's deck.

Apron — A kind of false, or inner stem, fitted exactly to the after side of the stem, to strengthen it. A keelson (see "Keelson") is also sometimes called an apron.

Backed (i.e., *"backed foreyards"*) — Reinforced to windward by additional stays (see "Stays").

Backstays — Long ropes or guys extending backwards from the heads of the masts and fastened to the side of the ship.

Ballast — Weight carried by a ship to ensure proper stability. When a ship is *in ballast,* she is without cargo and laden only with ballast.

Bark — A three-masted vessel which is fore-and-aft rigged (like a sport sailing boat) on the mizzenmast, and square rigged on the other masts, a mizzenmast being the rearmost mast of a three-masted vessel.

Battens — A strip of wood (or iron) used to fasten the edges of the tarpaulin with which a hatch is covered. To *batten down the hatches* is to nail strips of wood around the edges of the tarpaulin.

Belaying pin — A wooden pin or cleat around which a turn may be made with a rope to make the rope fast. That is, to hold the rope, or a line, secure.

Belly — That part of a sail which swells out when filled with wind.

Bending sails — Securing the sails to a yard or other spar.

Bilge stringers — Long, horizontal timbers that connect the lower part of the uprights in a ship's frame and support the floor above the bilge, the bilge being the bottom part of a ship's hull.

Binnacle — The frame or case on the deck of a ship in front of the helmsman which contains the ship's compass. The binnacle is fitted with a light (a whale oil lamp in Captain Barry's day) to illuminate the compass at night.

Block — A frame of wood or steel within which sheaves or pulleys are fitted, over which a rope may be led.

Boom — A long pole or spar used to extend the foot of a fore-and-aft sail.

Bow cants — Pieces of timber that support the bulkheads at the forward end of a ship.

Bowsprit — A large spar projecting forward from the ship's bow.

Brace (verb) — To swing or turn around by means of braces, a brace (noun) being a rope rove through a block at the end of a yard to swing it horizontally.

Brace the yards — To swing the yards (spars).

Brig — A vessel with two masts, both of them square rigged.

Brigantine — A two-masted vessel, square rigged on both masts, but with a fore-and-aft mainsail.

Capstan — An apparatus for raising and lowering a weight such as an anchor. It consists of a drum or cylinder revolving on an upright spindle. The drum is made to revolve by manpower applied to movable bars inserted in sockets around the top of the drum. The bars are pushed by men who walk around and around the capstan.

Caulkers — The men in a shipyard who caulk, which means to stop up the seams between the planks of a ship by driving oakum, or the like, into the cracks between planks. Melted pitch is often poured on afterward to prevent leaking.

Chafing gear — Mats or soft substances such as rope yarn and spun yarn fastened on the rigging and spars of a ship at strategic points to prevent rubbing and chafing.

Cotton, short staple — A variety of cotton with a short, fine fiber, which is considered superior to other varieties.

Crosstrees — The horizontal members of the topmast heads, which serve to extend the topmast rigging and provide a place for seamen to stand.

Deadeye — A round, laterally flattened wooden block encircled by a rope or iron band and pierced with three holes through which pass the lanyards that are used to extend the shrouds and stays in a ship's rigging.

Dubbers — To dub (a verb) in the days when wooden ships were built meant to trim with an adze. Dubbers were the men in a shipyard who used an adze to trim planks and timbers.

Faired — Past tense of the verb "fair," which is to make fit, or shape, according to the curvature of a ship.

False keel — The keel, which is the principal longitudinal member of a ship, is almost invariably located on the outside of the hull. A false keel is an extra piece which is often fastened to the bottom of the main keel to protect it.

Fasteners — The men in a shipyard who fasten the planks, boards, and other pieces to the vessel's frame.

Flying jib — A sail set outside the jib on an extension of the jib boom.

Footrope — A rope to which the lower edge of a sail is sewed. A footrope is also a rope extended under the bowsprit and other spars for the seamen to stand upon when reefing, furling, or making sail.

Forecastle — The large cabin where the sailors live and sleep in the forward part of a ship, under the forecastle head.

Forecastle head — A short, raised deck at the forward part of a ship.

Foreyard — The lowest yard on the foremast (See "Yard").

Futtock — One of the middle timbers of the frame of a ship between the floor and the top timbers.

Gaff — A staff armed with an iron hook. In another meaning of the word, a gaff is a spar used to extend the upper edge of fore-and-aft sails which are not set on stays.

Gale (whole gale) — In the terminology of sailing ship men, gales are classified as follows: A "moderate gale" is a wind between 32 and 38 miles per hour (28-33 knots); a "fresh gale" is a wind between 39 and 46 miles per hour (34-40 knots); and a "whole gale" is a wind between 55 and 63 miles an hour (48-55 knots). Winds stronger than a whole gale are either storms or hurricanes, depending upon the wind velocity. It should be noted that the United States Weather Bureau, today, uses a different classification. Winds from 39 to 54 miles an hour (34-47 knots) are simply "gales." Winds from 55 to 75 miles an hour (48-65 knots) are "whole gales." Winds above 75 miles an hour (65 knots) are "hurricanes."

Gasket — One of several bands of canvas, small lines, or ropes used to bind the sails to the yards, gaffs, or masts when the sails are furled.

Gauger — A man who gauges, measures, or counts the cargo as it is being loaded or unloaded.

Gear — The ropes, blocks, and other parts of the rigging that belong to a particular sail or spar. Broadly speaking, a ship's gear comprises all of the working parts and appliances on the ship.

Halyards — Ropes used to hoist yards, sails, and flags.

Headsails — Any sail set forward of the foremast, such as a jib or forestaysail (see sketch, "Sails of a Full-Rigged Ship," page 188).

Helmsman — The man at the wheel, or helm, of a ship, who steers the ship.

Jib — A triangular sail set upon a stay extending from the head (top) of the foremast to the bowsprit or jib boom.

Jib boom — A spar or boom extending from the bowsprit.

Johnathon — The term "Jonathon" originated as a nickname used by the British prior to the American Revolution to designate American patriots, New Englanders in particular. In time, it became the nickname for any American, a use of the word which is occasionally heard, even today. Herein it refers to a Yankee ship. During the American political campaigns of the mid-19th Century period, a Johnathon was an anti-slavery person, as well as one who was not against the immigration of foreigners.

Jolly boat — A boat of medium size belonging to a ship and used for general rough or small work.

Keel — The principal timber or combination of plates extending from stem to stern at the extreme bottom of the ship and supporting the whole frame of the ship.

Keelson — A longitudinal structural member incorporated with the frame of a ship to stiffen it, especially a structure of this type which is fastened to the keel.

Lanyard — A piece of rope for fastening something in a ship. A lanyard is also one of the pieces (ropes) passing through deadeyes that is used to extend the shrouds or stays.

Lead line — A weighted line (rope) with knots and/or markers spaced one fathom (six feet) apart that is used in making soundings.

Leadsman — A man who stands at the bow of a ship and uses a lead line to take soundings and thus determine the depth of the water through which the ship is passing.

List — To careen, heel, or incline to one side.

Log — Record of a ship's daily progress. (Also, see "Throwing a Log.")

Longboat — The largest boat belonging to a vessel.

Main topsail — See sketch, "Sails of a Full-Rigged Ship," page 188.

Man-of-war — A vessel equipped for warfare; any armed ship belonging to a recognized navy of a country.

Masthead — The top of a mast, especially of the lower mast.

Mizzen — A fore-and-aft sail set on the mizzenmast.

Mizzenmast — The aftermost mast in a two-masted and three-masted vessel. It is the third mast in a vessel having four or more masts.

Muzzle — To take in the sails.

Oakum — Old ropes untwisted and picked into loose fibers and used for caulking the seams of a ship, for stopping leaks. Oakum is often impregnated with tar.

Palm — A metal disc worn on the palm of the hand and used to push a needle through canvas when sewing sails.

Parceling (noun) — Spun yarn or long, narrow strips of canvas that are wound about a line or rope to exclude moisture.

Parceling (verb) — Parceling is to wind a strip of canvas spirally around a rope with the lay of the rope. The canvas is heavily tarred, after which the rope is served (see "Serving").

Payed — Smeared or covered with pitch, tar, tallow, or the like to keep out water and dampness.

Pilot — A man familiar with the local waters who conducts a ship into or out of a harbor or through a difficult channel or waterway.

Pointing — Tying up a reef in a sail with short pieces of flat, braided cord attached to the lower edge of the sail.

Poop — The stern or aftermost part of a ship, or, as used in this book, a deck above the ordinary deck in the aftermost part of the ship. In this sense, the word "poop" is short for "poop deck."

Poop deck — See "poop" above.

Port — The left side of a ship, when looking from aft to the bow.

Portuguese man-of-war — Any of several large siphonophores of the genus *Physalia* which have a large bladderlike pneumatophore with a sail-like crest on its upper side, by means of which they float at the surface of the sea.

Preventer stays — Auxiliary ropes used during periods of very strong wind to support a mast, leading from the head of the mast to some other mast or spar, or to some other part of the ship.

Punt — A long flat-bottomed boat with square ends, propelled with a pole or oars.

Put down (i.e., "put the helm down") — When steering, to turn the ship into the wind. In an emergency, putting helm down will quickly and effectively kill all forward speed of the ship.

Quarter, the — "The quarter" is an abbreviation for "quarterdeck," the quarter-deck being that part of the upper deck between the stern of a vessel and the aftermast. It was often used as a promenade for the ship's officers and passengers. Originally, the quarter-deck was a smaller deck above the half deck, which covered about a quarter of a vessel.

Ratline — One of the small, transverse ropes attached to the shrouds of a vessel to form a rope ladder by means of which sailors can climb aloft to work on the sails and yards.

Reef (verb) — To take reefs in sails, thereby reducing the size of the sail by rolling or folding a part of the sail and securing it by tying "reef points" about it (see "Pointing").

Reeve — To pass a rope or line through a hole, ring, or block.

Rigging — The ropes, chains, and cables that are employed to support and work all the masts, yards, and sails of a ship.

Roadstead — A protected place where ships may ride at anchor.

Rope walk — A long, covered walk, building, or room where ropes are manufactured.

Royal jib — See sketch, "Sails of a Full-Rigged Ship," page 188.

Royal studding sail — See sketch, "Sails of a Full-Rigged Ship," page 188.

Royal yard — The spar or yard from which the royal sails are suspended.

Royals — Small, square sails, usually the highest on the ship. The royals are carried on the royal yards and used only in a light breeze. See sketch, " Sails of a Full-Rigged Ship," page 188.

Running gear — The blocks, tackles, and other moving parts used on shipboard when a vessel is underway.

Running rigging — The running rigging comprises all the ropes hauled upon to brace the yards and make or take in sail.

Schooner — A fore-and-aft rigged vessel having two masts with the smaller sail on the foremast and with the mainmast stepped amidships.

Seizing — The operation of fastening together a lashing with small cord, generally tarred. Also the cord or lashing used for this purpose. A seizing binds ropes together or to other objects, more or less permanently.

Serve — To wind spun yarn, canvas, wire, or cord tightly around a rope to protect it from chafing.

Serving — A "serving" is applied after parceling a rope (see "Parceling"). Tarred marline is tightly wound about the rope, against the lay of the rope. The act of worming, parceling, and serving is referred to as "service," and it is applied to keep moisture from penetrating a rope. Its use is generally confined to the standing rigging.

Sextant — An instrument for navigation. A sextant is used for measuring the angular distance of two stars or other objects, or the altitude of the sun or other celestial bodies above the horizon.

Short staple cotton — See "Cotton, short staple."

Sheet — A line or rope for extending or controlling the angle of a sail.

Shrouds — Strong ropes extending from a ship's mastheads to each side of the ship to support the masts. The shrouds are a part of the standing rigging.

Sloop — A fore-and-aft rigged vessel with one mast and a single headsail jib.

Spanker — The aftersail of a ship or bark. It is a fore-and-aft sail extended by a boom and gaff from the after side of the mizzenmast.

Spar — A timber upon which the sails of a ship are bent, as a yard, boom, or gaff.

Spider — An iron outrigger to keep tackle blocks clear of a ship's side.

Spindrift — Sea spray.

Splicing — Uniting two ropes or parts of a rope by interweaving the strands.

Spun yarn — A line or cord of rope yarns twisted together and used to wrap around ropes to prevent the ropes from chafing.

Square sails — Sails extended horizontally on a yard secured to the mast, as opposed to fore-and-aft sails extended by means of stays, gaffs, or booms. The top edge of a square sail is called the "head" of the sail; the lower edge is called the "foot" of the sail.

Standing rigging — that rigging on a ship which is set up permanently, such as shrouds, stays, backstays, and the like.

Starboard — The right hand side of a ship, looking forward from the aft part of the ship.

Stays — Large, strong ropes used to support a mast by extending from the head of a mast down to some other mast or to some part of the ship. A stay is, in effect, a guy rope. There are fore and aft stays and backstays.

Steam box — The large wooden box in a shipyard in which planks are steamed to make them pliable for bending.

Stem — The timber at the bow of a ship to which the ends of the side planks are fastened.

Stemson — A piece of carved lumber bolted (or fastened with treenails) to the stem and keelson of a ship's frame near the bow.

Step (noun) — The block of wood in which the heel of a mast or a capstan is fixed, or "stepped."

Step (verb) — To fix the foot of a mast in its "step" and then erect the mast.

Sternpost — A more or less upright beam, rising from the after end of the keel and supporting the rudder of a ship.

Studding sail — See sketch, "Sails of a Full-Rigged Ship," page 188.

Taffrail — The aftermost portion of the rail around the poop deck of a ship.

Tare and tret — Tare is a deduction of weight made in allowance for the weight of the container in which an item of a ship's cargo is packaged. In the 19th Century, tret meant an allowance made to purchasers of certain articles for the waste or refuse after the tare was deducted.

Throwing a log — A log is an apparatus for ascertaining the rate of a ship's motion. It consists of a thin quadrant of wood, loaded so it will float upright, fastened to a line wound on a reel. In use, a sailor at the stern of a vessel "throws the log" overboard. As the log trails in the water behind the vessel, it pulls the line to which it is attached from the reel that the sailor holds in his hand. The sailor notes the time required for a marked known length of line to follow the log overboard. This determined, he can then readily calculate the forward speed of the ship.

Timber strake — The breadth or width of the planks along the bottom or sides of a vessel, reaching from stem to stern.

Tin knocker — Colloquial 19th-Century slang for a tinsmith; a worker in tin.

Top — A sort of platform surrounding the head of a lower mast on all sides.

Topgallant — See sketch, "Sails of a Full-Rigged Ship," page 188.

Topmast — The top half of the complete mast. It is a second mast fastened to the lower mast to make the mast taller.

Topsail — See sketch, "Sails of a Full-Rigged Ship," page 188.

Topsail schooner — A schooner with topsails (see "Schooner").

Treenail — A wooden peg, ordinarily of dry timber, which is driven into a hole drilled for it to fasten a plank to a timber, or to fasten two timbers together, when building a ship. After it has been driven in place, the dry treenail is moistened to make it swell and hold fast. Treenails were often called "trunnels."

Trunnel — See "Treenail," above.

Unlay — To untwist a rope.

Waist — The horizontal middle portion of a ship's upper deck.

Watch — The period of time occupied by each work section of a ship's crew while on duty. Each half of the crew usually stood alternate watches.

"Weather the main braces" — A command which directs the sailors to pull on the main braces (see "Braces") to swing the yards to the angle that will obtain the maximum effect of the wind on the sails.

Winch — A hoisting machine in which a drum that serves as a reel for rope or cable is turned by a crank. In modern times, winches are often operated by steam, gasoline, or electric power.

Worming — Worming is the laying in of small stuff (string or cord) between the strands of a rope to fill the spaces between the strands and make the rope smooth. Worming prepares a rope for "parceling" (see "Parceling").

Yard — A long spar, tapered toward the ends and set athwart a mast to support and spread the head of a square sail.

BIBLIOGRAPHY

In addition to the letters of Captain Charles E. Barry and the usual standard encyclopedias and atlases, the following publications were used as sources of information in preparing the material from which this book was written:

American Review. "Railway Passenger Travel, 1825-80" (Scotia, New York: 1962).

Angas, Commander W. Mack. *Rivalry on the Atlantic* (New York: Lee Furman, Inc., 1939).

Anglesey Tourist Association. The *Anglesey Official County Handbook* (Llangefni, Wales).

Barry, William E. *Sketch of an Old River* (Boston: Alfred Mudge and Sons, 1888).

Bryant, S. E. *A List of Vessels Built in Kennebunk* (Kennebunk, Maine: compiled in 1874. Published by The Brick Store Museum, 1950).

Clark, George Edward. *Seven Years in a Sailor's Life* (Boston: Adams and Co., 1867).

Corliss, Carlton J. *Main Line of Mid-America* (New York: Creative Age Press, 1950).

Dane, Walter L. and Charles E. Renich. *History of Kennebunk* (Privately printed, 1911).

Fairburn, William Armstrong. *Merchant Sail* Vols. I-VI (Center Lowell, Mass.: Fairburn Marine Educational Foundation, Inc., 1944-55).

Gilpatrick, George A. *Kennebunk History* (Kennebunk, Maine: The Star Print, 1939).

Holbrook, Stewart H. *The Story of American Railroads* (New York: Crown Publishers, 1947).

Huchins, G. B. *The American Maritime Industries and Public Policy* (Cambridge, Mass.: Harvard University Press, 1941).

Jones, Herbert G. *The Kings Highway from Portland to Kittery* (Freeport, Maine: The Bond Wheelwright Company, 1961).

Miller, William. *A New History of the United States* (New York: George Braziller, Inc., 1958).

Morison, Samuel Eliot. *The Maritime History of Massachusetts* (Boston: Houghton, Mifflin Co., 1921).

Rowe, William H. *Ancient North Yarmouth and Yarmouth, Maine* (Yarmouth, Maine: The Southworth-Anthoensen Press, 1937).

- - - - - *The Maritime History of Maine* (New York: W. W. Norton & Co., 1948).

Saltonstall, William G. "Just Ease Her When She Pitches," *The American Neptune Quarterly Journal of Maritime History* (October, 1955) Salem Mass.: The American Neptune, Inc.

Smith, Philip Chadwick Foster. "Crystal Blocks of Yankee Coldness," *Essex Institute Historical Collections* (July, 1961). Wenham, Mass.: Wenham Historical Association, Reprint, 1962.

State Street Trust Company. *Old Shipping Days in Boston* (Boston: 1918).

Thompson, Margaret J. *Captain Nathinel Lord Thompson and the Ships He Built* (Boston: Charles E. Lauriat Co., 1937).

Villiers, Alan. *The Way of a Ship* (New York: Charles Scribner Sons, 1953).

- - - - - "Ships Through the Ages," *National Geographic Magazine*, (April, 1963).

Wheatley, Wilkins W. *Square Riggers Before the Wind* (New York: E. P. Dutton, 1939).

Winsor, Justin, ed. *The Memorial History of Boston* Volume IV (Boston: Tichnor and Company, 1881).

MARINE CHARTS USED.

United States Department of Commerce Charts:
        Massachusetts Bay
        Boston Harbor
        Savannah River and Wassaw Sound
U. S. Navy Hydrographic Office Charts:
        Chart of the World, #H.O. 1262-A
        India — West Coast, Bombay Harbor
        Coast of India, Arnala Island to Khanderi, including Bombay Harbor
        River Hooghly — Sagar Roads to Calcutta
        British Isles — Holyhead to Armes Head